# The Battle of
# the Books

*Two Decades of Irish Cultural Debate*

## W. J. Mc CORMACK

THE LILLIPUT PRESS

First published in 1986 by
THE LILLIPUT PRESS LTD
Gigginstown, Mullingar,
Co. Westmeath, Ireland


*British Library Cataloguing in Publication Data*
The battle of the books: two decades of
Irish cultural debate
1. English literature — Irish authors
— History and criticism  2. Criticism —
History — 20th century
I. Title
820.9'9415      PR8755

ISBN 0-946640-13-0


Cover design by Jarlath Hayes
Set in 11 on 13 Bembo by
Koinonia Ltd of Manchester
and printed in England by
Richard Clay Ltd
of Bungay, Suffolk

# Contents

# Preface

The argument which follows was written immediately after my return to Ireland in the autumn of 1985. I had spent the previous year in the United States of America, and in attempting to settle back into Dublin, I was befriended by Antony Farrell of The Lilliput Press. In the course of what became regular Thursday evening exchanges, plans for *The Battle of the Books* emerged. Without his contribution to those exchanges, the thing would never have been written.

During the autumn and winter months, a pamphlet originally intended grew to be the present small book. What had been planned exclusively as a critical reading of the disputes revolving round the *Field Day* company's various projects soon gave evidence of requiring at least a modicum of historically alert reflection. Three moments have been acknowledged as especially relevant. First, there is the 'Indian spring' of the 1960s, summarized here within the career of Conor Cruise O'Brien. (I define an Indian spring as breezy barometric readings followed by an atrocious summer.) Second, there is a period which we will call Edwardian, though it should be interpreted as beginning earlier than 1901, lasting longer than Edward's reign, and including certainly the Irish baptism in the Somme. In this connection, see my comments on criticism in Ulster, including *Field Day*. Third, there is the (anti)revolutionary decade of the 1790s, significant in that it gave rise to key terms of social description (and prescription) subsequently thought to be far more antique in their origins. Here, resistance to an altered interpretation can be seen as revealing a variety of hitherto concealed interests, though I should concede at the outset that the altered interpretation is my own and that I may have mis-measured the resistance accordingly. Having noted these three historical moments, and still emphasizing their importance for contemporary criticism, I stick to the original emphasis on our current cultural debates.

As the typescript grew so did the publisher's support – a generous response, rare among publishers. Moreover the delay in completion allowed Ciaran Brady to read through the work, and the result has been the elimination of many infelicities and inaccuracies. Battles should not be dedicated to friends, new friends especially, but in now completing *The Battle of the Books* I nonetheless want to acknowledge warmly the support of both of the friends named above.

*W.J.M.*
*September 1986*

# 1 Remembering *Atlantis* (1970–1974)

*art does not extirpate myth; it merely assuages it.*

Theodor W. Adorno

SOME TIME in 1969 Seamus Deane read his poems in a pottery-shed at the back of Trinity College, Dublin. Derek Mahon and I were in the audience, and when the reading was over we got together with Deane. One thing led to another. Irish literary magazines at that time were a strange collection: at one end of the scale there was the genteel provincialism of *The Dublin Magazine,* at the other the wildly experimental (but physically frail) *Broadsheet* published by Hayden Murphy. Northern Ireland had given birth to *The Honest Ulsterman,* a journal which displayed its honesty by removing the sub-title 'a handbook for revolution' at the request of the police. (An editorial explained D. H. Lawrence's revolution had been intended.) Beyond those, a poet had to rely on the books page of a few newspapers for an outlet in Ireland. There was even less in the way of a critical or speculative journal. The only public discussion of literature, culture, and ideas generally, took place in book reviews: Irish book reviews were, and are, opportunities for banality, dishonesty and lachrymose idiocy.

What we had in mind was a journal, resembling *Encounter* in format, *The Transatlantic Review* in tone. Each of us, Deane, Mahon and myself, had plenty of ideas as to what we wanted to publish. We had little or no experience of publishing or business in any shape or form. Two further prospective editors joined the team – Michael Gill of the old Dublin publishing family (now operating under the name of Gill & Macmillan); and Augustine Martin, a lecturer like Deane in University College, whose strong point was a canny knowledge of what the Irish educational world would stomach in the way of intellectual innovation. The collective genius of three poets, the professional skill of a publisher and the diplomacy of Mr Martin were thought a sure formula for success.

Almost from the outset it was also a formula for disagreement. An article on Francis Stuart – probably not a very good one in retrospect, but bringing a neglected novelist before a new readership – was dropped to make room for a piece by Denis Donoghue. Behind the scenes such decisions were inevitable, but the public image of *Atlantis* was one of cheerfulness and universal toleration. Austin Clarke, Conor Cruise O'Brien and Denis Donoghue were among the magazine's official patrons. Samuel Beckett, Donald Davie and Brian Moore were among its first sponsors (the ones who put up the money). Virtually every Irish writer of the day appeared somewhere in the six issues between March 1970 and the spring of 1974: Francis Stuart, John Banville, J.G. Farrell and Aidan Higgins; Thomas Kinsella, Seamus Heaney, John Montague and Michael Hartnett; Desmond Hogan and Gerard Dawe, all found a place in its pages. Commentary on political and related matters came from Liam de Paor, Desmond Fennell, Terence Brown and Roy Johnston. Nor was the emphasis exclusively Irish. Much of the sixth issue was devoted to literature from eastern Europe – East Germany, Romania and the Soviet Union. French poets in translation included Yves Bonnefoy, Robert Desnos, Jacques Dupin and Jules Supervielle. Extracts from Walter Jens's *Die Gotten sind Sterblich* were translated by Martyn Bond. Jim O'Malley contributed the first full translation of Luigi Pirandello's essay on humour. Add to this essays by Stephen Heath and Phillip Pettit, two contributions from Donoghue and one from Cruise O'Brien – all in six issues – and you have a fair account of our range.

Yet from the outset this bumptious cornucopia was perilously balanced. The first editorial included such ringing questions as

Adorno died last August. Who cares? We have a depopulated West and a rancid North. Is there any parallel elsewhere which can make those situations more intelligible? Name six Irish painters living or dead.

Though the magazine devoted an entire issue (no. 5, April 1973) to the concept of a New Ireland, the desire for a comparative attitude to the problems of northern (and southern) Ireland never acquired the name of action. Indeed, one of the general tendencies of the period under consideration throughout these pages has been this failure to see Irish affairs in relation to anything else, anywhere. By the time the final issue appeared the editorial tone had become discernibly more sombre:

Despite the speed with which public affairs develop and mature, we have little confidence that, by the time this issue of *Atlantis* reaches the public, Ireland will have significantly advanced in its politics.

The editorial then proceeded to warn two northern politicians (Paddy Devlin and Gerry Fitt) of the dangers for radicals inherent in participating in coalition governments – at least that aspect of policy was justified! It concluded by presenting the literature of eastern Europe as a sort of implicit comparison for Ireland, adding some observations on the direful quality of what fiction had been written from the Troubles and contrasting the role of the short story and prose poem in East Germany and elsewhere.

There were of course various reasons for the close-down of *Altantis*. One quite simply was the vast increase in printing and paper costs at the beginning of the seventies: *Atlantis* had been all too handsomely designed (cover by Derek Bell) and fastidiously printed by Liam Miller's Dolmen Press. These standards simply could not be maintained, and it seemed better to close – perhaps temporarily – than to degrade the magazine's entire style of presentation. Moreover, by the end of 1971 the editors found themselves no longer living near each other down by the Liffey-side. Derek Mahon had moved to London, while I had gone to teach at Magee College in Derry. (Only Deane, a Derryman, remained in Dublin.) Editorial correspondence, replacing convivial editorial conference, tended to bring out differences of opinion or priority. In my own case, the frustration of putting together a journal which carried an editorial already two to three months out of date when it reached the newsstands was acute. Living in Derry, I was particularly struck by the gap between day-to-day experience and whatever reflection upon it *Atlantis* might venture. Looking back on things, I am now half persuaded that a medium for reflection was so badly needed at that crucial early stage of the Troubles that publication ought to have been maintained

11

even at the expense of appearing temporarily out-stripped by the nine o'clock news. But reflection was not as obviously urgent then as it is now, and all the other factors urged the common sense of closing-down. The sales record (despite Mr Martin's way with the nuns) did not encourage any other course. The possibility that *Atlantis* might be taken over as a prestige 'house journal' disappeared as it became evident that the editorial line diverged from the conventional wisdom of the day. Our first editorial had begun, 'This magazine did not exist, so it was necessary to invent it.' Its epitaph might ultimately be, 'Badly needed, it failed to exist.'

Though other magazines took up some of its interests, nothing has ever replaced it. *Cyphers* and more recently *Tracks* have encouraged translations from a diversity of sources. *The Crane Bag* inherited the investigative role, making a regular feature of special issues on special topics. The distinctive blend of cosmopolitanism, radicalism and chic, which had been the *Atlantis* trademark, has disappeared. As I have said, one reason for its disappearance is that the reality of its existence was, even at the time, uncertain. Many of the contributions were 'once-off' things, impossible to repeat but giving the impression of far-flung international connections and hitherto unsuspected wells of native genius. The radicalism was tacit until events challenged it. The chic was more expensive than the Irish market could bear. A magazine which included Conor Cruise O'Brien and Denis Donoghue in its opening number could only do so in style. Without the style, the tensions became all too obvious.

The editorial warning about coalition governments touched on the political activities of the magazine's best-known patron. Not surprisingly, the controversies of the 1970s were built into *Atlantis*. There had been the very faintest warning of this development even when the magazine was still at the planning stage. Among the names chosen as potential patrons had been Sean O'Faolain's, and in writing to him we drew a parallel between our own objective and his own, earlier, magazine. Dr O'Faolain declined to join us. The harmony of literature and good causes, which O'Faolain and *The Bell* had achieved in the forties, was to prove elusive in the seventies.

12

And the future? Controversy and turbulence have been the customary handmaids of literature in Ireland. The author of *The Faerie Queene* had his house burned behind his heels. Maria Edgeworth visited her publisher in prison. Yeats was 'a paramilitary'. Joyce had his works banned in the English-speaking world and burnt in the Third Reich. Frank O'Connor, Sean O'Faolain and Francis Stuart soldiered in the war of independence or the civil war which followed. Samuel Beckett wrote *Watt* in Vichy France, alternating as *maquis* agent. By comparison the present generation of writers have lived in peace and prosperity, more troubled by the anomalies of their exemption from income tax than by the prospects of prison or sudden death by gunshot or hangman's rope. Occasionally an odd, regressive individual on the Left festoons the Arts Council railings with papal cartoons of Samuel Beckett (minus his *croix de guerre)* and with other rubbish, choosing a time when striking dustbinmen were assailed by the armed forces of the State.

Despite the evidence of complacency and struggling egoism, it is the present generation of writers who have lived through the longest period of violent conflict in Ireland. The conflict of course has been for the most part confined to working-class areas of Belfast and to isolated pockets of rural intransigence. Writers, for the most part middle-class in their manner of living if not in their origins, are only occasionally touched by the violent routine of their fellow-citizens' lives. Controversy and turbulence are not synonymous of course: many of the disputes about Yeats and Joyce seem unconnected with a turbulent society – did the author of *Finnegans Wake* really remain faithful to Mother Church, despite appearances? Was Yeats really of aristocratic stock, or just middle class (like everyone else)? In the last fifteen years, however, even these finicking problems of definition have acquired kinetic political effects. Around Joyce there has grown a new sense of the inevitably political character of all writing. Critics investigating Yeats have found themselves confronted with the complicated quesion of Irish Protestant 'identity' as currently hyperactive in Ulster.

The present Troubles began very shortly after Seamus Heaney published his first collection of poems, *Death of a Naturalist* (1966). For several years it was felt that the latest outbreak of political violence was just another periodic and temporary disruption of normality. Not until the end of the 1970s did it really dawn on the plain people of Ireland that this *is* normality now. For some, the response has been to acknowledge the violence of the present as irrefutable evidence of an inescapable past, a past which determines the present whether through the agency of British policy, republican tactics, or loyalist rhetoric. Not many have considered the possibility that violence in Irish society – in Dublin or Belfast, political in its vocabulary or otherwise – is part of a broader pattern in Western society. The result has been that the debate on Irish affairs is conducted in a remarkably inward fashion – even the term 'the Troubles' carries with it a sense of intimate possession. Unlike gangsterism, mugging, or 'the consequences of alienation within a decaying urban environment', your Troubles are your own. Only the Italians with their Cosa Nostra rival the Irish in the possession of their unhappiness. Despite this recent realization of the likely permanence of violence, most Irish writers continue to regard the Troubles as a distinct and isolatable phenomenon, to be dealt with or otherwise at will. While this may strike readers in more sophisticated (and equally violent) parts of the world as naïve, one positive benefit has been the highly explicit discussion of the relation between literature and politics. The paradox then is this: a culture which assumes a simplistic relation between these two artificially isolated areas is nonetheless capable of discussing the relationship itself in a remarkably accessible way. In Great Britain, any similar debate would either be marginalized as a peculiar preoccupation of the Left, or enfolded in archaic and neoplatonic reverence for an England long since disappeared.

Things are different in Ireland, where the Left (to use a helpful if vague term) is weak and disorganized, and where neoplatonic reverence is concentrated on the existing landscape. (Irish poetry is incurably descriptive, despite the general indifference of the public and the authorities to the appearance of their environment.) In the course of these pages I hope to trace the growth of this vigorous, if at times crude, debate. But the material will reach far beyond the frontiers of literary criticism as normally defined in the Anglo-American world. Most of the leading participants will be poets and playwrights, as well as critics. More crucially, the very nature and definition of the State (indeed two States) is inextricably linked to the various critical stances adopted. This might be contested by some who regard their critical activities as wholly contained within the realm of literature, but the very notion of such a 'realm' is itself a political gesture, whether of retreat or defiance. For readers in Chicago there is the novelty here of considering a culture in which the events of the street are not relegated to the domain of trivia. For readers in Manchester there is the even greater novelty of considering a culture in which the nods and winks on which their own State is founded come under articulate scrutiny.

Early in his career Jonathan Swift took up the controversy between the Ancients and Moderns in scholarship, and satirized the warring factions in *The Battle of the Books*. His mock-heroic device is brilliantly deployed as the various learned tomes and weighty treatises scramble down off the shelves to fight it out on the floor of the Saint James library. Would that I had the skill to up-date that ancient device, presenting Edna Longley as a trusty traditional Remington assailing the colourful graphics of Dr Atari Kiberd! Or I might relate how Cruise O'Brien, paper-shredder, set about the *Collected Floppy Discs* of Seamus Deane.

Something other than skill prevents such an approach. In 1986 the echo of Swift's title is not mock-heroic only. It catches the actual vocabulary of Ian Paisley and Charles Haughey, not to mention the paramilitaries and the Special Air Services: the battle of the books may well preface an actual battle. And if that battle develops – it has been taking place in fragmentary fashion for well over sixteen years – then the poets and critics will have contributed something to the conflict. I don't suggest that some direct responsibility will be theirs, but I would argue that the issues in dispute have for many generations been given their characteristic formulations in quasi-literary terms. The Republic of Ireland was launched by a rebellion of (mediocre) poets; Seamus Heaney left Northern Ireland in 1972 partly at least because his growing reputation as a poet was seen by Protestant extremists as a dangerous instance of insubordination in one of those whom they regarded as lesser beings. There is a sense in which Northern Ireland, with the unique constitutional arrangements which have been built up around it, exemplifies the conventions of Practical Criticism – nothing extrinsic to the 'text' of Northern Ireland is allowed to impinge on the integrity of that cultural artefact. For many years the mother of parliaments (Westminster) was prohibited from discussing the blatant malpractices of the government in Northern Ireland. To travesty a phrase of Archibald MacLeish's, it was felt that Ulster should not Mean, but Be. If its being were now to take a bloodier and more overtly violent form, those who practise writing in Ireland would no more find themselves exempt from the battle than they have been exempt from recent criticism.

Ulster, though not a state, had a government: in similarly overdetermined fashion Ulster, though neither homogeneously Protestant in itself nor the homeland of all Protestants in Ireland, was cast as the Protestant Cause. This is not mere gerrymandering nor the impercipience of lusty enthusiasts; it is a concrete, actual and historically prolonged experiment in the politics which arise from a totalitarian philosophy equating ontology and identity, Being and Belonging. Throughout the long narrative of Ulster government, no reflective, self-critical writer in Ulster uttered more than a valedictory groan at this condition. If there have been manifestations of a similar kind in the Irish Republic – and there have – several crucial distinguishing factors should be noted. First, neither government nor quasi-government ever fell to such powers. Second, a modicum of self-critical awareness did pervade southern intellectual life, and with publicly acknowledged effects.

The literary culture of other countries always looks tidier than one's own. The notion of 'schools' or 'movements' seems either excessively neat or embarrassingly pretentious when applied to the 'scattering of incoherent lives' (Thomas Kin-

sella's still useful phrase) which is contemporary Irish literature. There was a curious maxim of Eamon de Valera's which
encouraged him to talk to his own people as if he were an
opponent, the better to acquaint them with the complexities
of his thought. Some similar strategy is required in the area
of literary disputation. Yet the classification which I have
willy-nilly introduced here is not entirely a fiction. From the
relative openness of *Atlantis* to the tightly structured team of
polemicists operating since 1983 under the name *Field Day*,
one traces the growth of alliances and antagonisms new to
Irish literary debate. It is well known that, in the past, Irish
cultural life had more than a few disputations, even riots. But
the lines of tension and opposition now have a more overtly
ideological quality – and this on all sides of the debate. The
eirenic Derek Mahon, reviewing a book by Terry Eagleton
which did not cry out for attention of any kind, is suddenly
caught up in uncharacteristic denunciations of intellectual
movements – not unlike a wanderer on some deserted
battlefield of yore stabbing at, cutting down, empty bushes.
*Field Day* is a useful focus for inquiries which will reach beyond
the activities of that formidable team, and light may be cast
on a nervousness which re-enacts a past it seeks to escape.

None of these enterprises in any way diminishes the vigour
of the opposition, who review a *Field Day* pamphlet as if it
were some edict imposed on defenceless readers by an unstable
and treacherous Fate. Thus, the lines of battle are drawn up
by kindly scholars and intelligent parents who are well aware
that other kinds of battle are under way. Moreover, the language of the debate is from the outset over-blown with a host
of short-hand terms – we love the short-hand as we despise
the long-head – Sunningdale, the Provos, Dyplock, Power-
Sharing, the Agreement. The outsider may believe that these
are precise, if difficult, terms he will eventually learn to use.
Certainly, they have something of the intimacy already noted
in 'the Troubles'. There is a kind of family slang at work, and
that suggests some sense of community or bonding, a sharing
of meaning. Yet at another level it is important to note that
these words are all hollow; they ring with vacancy and failure.

For the writer there is the additional problem that the language which is his only tool, his only material, his only skill, is being puffed and pulled beyond recognition. The debates between aesthetes and structuralists in England occasionally refer to the growth of a specialized jargon, jargon being the language of ideas the denouncer has rejected in advance. In Ireland criticism has tended to be rather amateur. Recently, however, denunciations are a great deal more frequent and embittered, and the cause of this is not an upsurge of personal spleen (though that exists too). To introduce a specialized terminology, whether from French post-structuralism or Critical Theory, is to challenge the comforting belief that community and bonding do survive, and that 'our people' proliferate. It is anxiously pretended that the language has come through the bombs and the bombast miraculously unscathed. The experience of the Germans after the Second World War, reflected in the poetry of Johannes Bobrowski and (more recently) in the criticism of George Steiner, has not been noted. If ever the violence of the streets and the scraggy hill-farms ceases, there will still be a desperate need for intelligent criticism in order to render the language capable of acknowledging that cessation.

# 2 The Mystery of the Clarity of Conor Cruise O'Brien

EARLY IN 1986 Conor Cruise O'Brien ended a long intermission in his career as writer, publishing a weighty account of the history and politics of modern Israel. Reviewing it with great sympathy and intelligence, George Steiner blundered in the final paragraph into a lament at the author's exclusion from the politics of his own tormented homeland. A murmur of gratified dissent rose from the armchairs of Ireland, for a benighted foreigner like Steiner could not be expected to recall Cruise O'Brien's *resignation* from Seanad Eireann following protests at his prolonged absenteeism as elected representative of Dublin University graduates. And so the legend of the Cruiser eats into the exposed surfaces of Irish intellectual life, deepening the impression of his name, reducing the material. Literary critic, government minister, newspaper editor, historian, playwright, international civil servant, Conor Cruise O'Brien gives every impression of being that *rara avis,* an Irish intellectual in the European mode. Yet his position today (and yesterday) is highly anomalous, as the murmuring armchairs testify. One synopsis might read: never has there been a good cause without Conor at its head. Another: never has there been a good cause without Conor taking to his heels. Both perhaps fail to do justice to the truth.

First, despite (perhaps because of) his many interests, he has never been at the head of anything in Ireland. Even his adversaries concede that he had contributed energetically to many areas of Irish life, but he has been for the most part a contributor rather than a leader, a member not a founder of movements. Many of these have failed to hold his interest. His departure from government was decided by the electorate, but the exclusion of which Steiner complained was ultimately self-inflicted. For many, he has gone through the familiar disenchantment with left-wing politics, a disenchantment intensified by his formidable powers as a controversialist. Yet an emphasis on this withdrawal from active political life in the Irish Republic misses much of significance in a career which started long before he joined his Labour colleagues in Liam Cosgrave's coalition cabinet.

If there is a pattern to the literary debates of the last two decades, the initiating moment can be traced even further back, and the process of tracing it adds to the excitement of the chase. O'Brien's first substantial contribution to public debate was presented under a pseudonym. That, together with the subject matter of the book, led to its being half-neglected in Ireland at the time, even though some of the material had first appeared in *The Bell*. In 1952, writing as Donat O'Donnell, he published *Maria Cross: Imaginative Patterns in a Group of Modern Catholic Writers*. Much of the material under examination was French: the fiction of François Mauriac, Georges Bernanos, and Léon Bloy; the drama of Paul Claudel, and the poetry of Charles Péguy. *Maria Cross* is a surer guide to the author's concerns than the better-known *Writers and Politics* (1965), which brought together reviews and articles published in the previous ten years. And it is likely to remain the sure guide, unless a projected biography of Edmund Burke supplants it. It would be too simple to say that Cruise O'Brien, after his political adventures, has now reverted to an older loyalty summarized in that first book's sub-title, but those who see O'Brien solely in terms of his alleged abandonment of socialism – was there a first embrace logically to preface the rejection? – fail to measure the brevity of his declarations.

A commitment certainly existed, on paper. The introduction to *Writers and Politics* (1965) opens boldly enough with a piece of dialogue:

'Are you a socialist?' asked the African leader.
  I said, yes.
  He looked me in the eye. 'People have been telling me', he said lightly, 'that you are a liberal. . .'
  The statement in its context invited a denial. I said nothing. (p. xiii)

Undoubtedly, the author has been wearied by citations of this declaration, but the entire strategy of the exchange is rife with complications. He writes that he said yes, leaving unwritten any divergence between what he said and what he believed. The African leader, on the other hand, has been decked out with an ironical quizzical style not unlike O'Brien's own – at times. It also bears a resemblance, in its mixture of bold direct speech and deft quasi-self-quotation, to the narrative of Meursault in *The Outsider,* as rendered in O'Brien's study of Albert Camus. After recording that he said nothing, he gives us nothing of the African leader's response. Has this been a dialogue at all? Has it not come to look like some kind of codified meditation, or monologue, of a less social kind?

While publishing the material collected in 1965, Dr O'Brien was pursuing two other careers. With *Parnell and his Party* (1957) he established himself as a talented historian of the Theodore Moody/F.S.L. Lyons school. Indeed, O'Brien was in many respects well in advance of the school in which he was trained, combining a breadth of general argument to which mastery of detail paid its due homage. Though basically an expanded version of his post-graduate research, the book has real links with the literary criticism of *Maria Cross,* especially through the essay on 'The Parnellism of Sean O'Faolain'. Though *To Katanga and Back* (1962) appears an exotic successor to an expanded doctoral thesis on party manoeuvres in the 1880s, it possesses the same flair for historically significant detail and the same seemingly crystal-clear mode of writing. There is something dream-like, on occasion, in the transparency of Dr O'Brien's prose – perhaps a tribute to the rigours of repression at work. In its global view of things the Katanga book has now been counterbalanced by *The Siege.*

The earlier book on the Congo serves an additional function – as a prominent marker in the author's second career. It was by virtue of his work as an Irish civil servant involved in foreign affairs that he had ended up as Dag Hammarskjold's personal UN representative in Katanga. Back in Dublin he had something of a reputation as an articulate opponent of Irish partition, and soon his exposure of British and Belgian machinations in west Africa only enhanced this local reputation. Early in the 1960s he looked very much the man of the moment, alert to the post-colonial problems of the Third

World, broadly sympathetic in his reading of literature, and eminently capable as a historical writer to draw these diverse concerns together. It was in this light that *Atlantis* had sought his support at the end of the decade.

*Parnell and his Party* was to prove to be his first and last academic publication, though *Maria Cross* should not be casually disregarded in this connection. His publications thereafter include numerous books in the general sense of the word, all of which carry something of the collaborative or occasional in their presentation. Two deserve particular attention in the context of the crisis which was to arise: in 1965 O'Brien published 'Passion and Cunning: an Essay on the Politics of W.B. Yeats' in a collection of essays to mark the centenary of the poet's birth; in 1970 the Fontana Modern Masters series issued his brief study of Camus, this linking back to the earlier interest in French fiction.

'Passion and Cunning' remains O'Brien's most significant and extensive contribution to literary debate in Ireland. In less than twenty thousand words, he ransacked Yeats's poetry and related writings to establish the highly strategic sense of politics which the poet possessed (and was possessed by). But more than this, he proceeded to lay bare the unequivocal sympathy with fascism which coloured Yeats's late career. The essay produced a storm of protest, though the only notable attempt at an academic refutation at the time came from Patrick Cosgrave, later to distinguish himself as Margaret Thatcher's mid-term biographer. Subsequent discussions have found 'Passion and Cunning' unavoidable, even by the tactic of ignoring some of Yeats's most resonantly political writings – 'Purgatory' and the poet's explication of it with reference to Nazi legislation. In a sense, then, O'Brien brought to Ireland a kind of analysis which was virtually unknown previously, an analysis which assumed a European context while yet reading the poetry with a discerning eye, an analysis which set out from no *a priori* separation of politics and poetics. In short, he was the forerunner of *Field Day,* even if neither party would care to acknowledge the relationship yet.

There is a complication with this 'seminal' essay, an aspect of it at least as characteristic of the author as its combative style. It is, virtually, incomplete. The final footnote advises that 'just as "The Second Coming" contains the rise of Fascism, I think that the mysterious and beautiful poem "Cuchulain Comforted" may contain the fall of Fascism. I hope in a separate essay to examine the themes of the four last poems' (p.278). That further essay has never, to the best of my knowledge, been written. If indeed Yeats's particular blend of politics and aesthetics did somehow include a critique of fascism, Dr O'Brien had declined to disinter it for public discussion. It may be that his critics, among the professional and confessional Yeatsians, have taken this silence as a tacit admission of defeat in the general project of extrapolating an underlying ideology from the body of poetry. In this they would be wrong; it seems more likely that the distaste for right-wing politics for the most part evident in 'Passion and Cunning' has abated. Having launched, however remotely in time, the revisionism of the *Field Day* team and the editors of *The Crane Bag,* Dr O'Brien left the field early. Perhaps an unregenerate, or unregenerated, Yeats has gradually become more acceptable to him. Their attitudes on several issues – Edmund Burke, the separateness of Northern Ireland – are reconcilable. It is typical of O'Brien's tangential manner of operating that the promise to look at Yeats's four last poems should not be left wholly neglected: nothing goes to waste. Five years later, writing of Camus's *The Outsider,* he describes the faceless Arab characters who silently reappear throughout that novel as 'working like the enigmatic shrouds in Yeats's "Cuchulain Comforted"'. He quotes (p. 26):

Eyes peered out of the branches and were gone.

Instead of a conclusive essay on Yeats, we get a digression in an essay on Camus. Conor Cruise O'Brien as critic is systematically discrete.

Yeats crops up on another occasion in the study of Camus. In the chapter on *The Fall* Dr O'Brien quotes the poem 'The Great Day', sees Camus in the first part of *The Rebel* as offering a different view of things (a view in which the beggar's revolt is approved), and proceeds to see the second and third parts of the book as drastically different. This shift in Camus is a shift towards an explicit anti-communism; at another level, it is a shift in the thinking of Conor Cruise O'Brien. His study of Camus is organized through the three novels. Perhaps the most illuminating pages are those in which he discusses the incipient religious allegiances of the third novel: once again there is an indirect cross-reference to the material of *Maria Cross*. The discussion of *The Plague,* on the other hand, throws light on much that has been unclear to date in Dr O'Brien's own thought.

O'Brien has commented on the curious role of the Arab population of Algeria, and sees in this role evidence of Camus's *colon* failure to regard the *colonisé* as genuinely real. (At this stage the novelist is very much the patronized beneficiary of the critic's 'rational humanism'.) But turning rather sharply on the responses of Germaine Brée, he mocks her contention that working-class districts might be less susceptible to racialism than a middle-class milieu. Even more sharply, he observes that 'a working-class population which would be "impervious to racial barriers" would be an unusual phenomenon'. No evidence, Irish, French or Algerian, is offered to substantiate this judgment, though it will play a crucial part in the subsequent analysis of *The Plague*.

At some level, *The Plague* is about the German occupation of France, about fascism: that much is agreed. Dr O'Brien, however, advances from this fairly elementary position with enthusiasm, to argue that the central characters of the novel (that is, middle-class Frenchmen living in Oran in eastern Algeria) 'were not devoted fighters against the plague: they were the plague itself' (p.48). This is an argument which the critic concedes would be 'distasteful' to many, including Camus. The critic's making it is thus all the more commendable; it exemplifies all that trenchant opposition to colonialism and imperialism for which Dr O'Brien had earned his own modest reputation for *sainteté laïque* in the early sixties. However, there is a sudden turn-about in this racial categorization right at the end of the chapter. Having announced early on that there was a view, not unappealing, according to which the real rats which caused the symbolic plague were the French 'colons', the chapter concludes:

Eight years after the publication of *The Plague* the rats came up to die in the cities of Algeria. To apply another metaphor of Camus's, the Algerian insurrection was 'the eruption of the boils and pus which had before been working inwardly in the society'. And this eruption came precisely from the quarter in which the narrator had refused to look: from the [Arab] houses which Dr Rieux never visited and from the conditions about which the reporter, Rambert, never carried out his enquiry. (pp. 50-51)

This is sufficiently clear, insufficiently 'discrete', to warrant a moment's further examination. There is no doubt that the houses in question *were* Arab houses – O'Brien himself quotes (pp. 46-47) a passage about the 'curiously deserted' native quarter, savours the above-quoted phrase by repeating it, adding the remark that 'neither Rieux, the doctor, nor Rambert, the reporter, ever goes into these houses' (p. 47). Finally, 'the source of the plague is what we pretend is not there and the preacher himself is already, without knowing it, infected by the plague' (p. 51). The critic remains silent on the second Algerian insurrection, the rebellion of the *pieds noirs* French Algerians against President de Gaulle's policy. Though *The Fall* is set in Amsterdam, this attitude towards the Arabs preoccupies O'Brien's treatment of Camus's last novel also.

There is a crucial ambiguity, indeed multivalency, in the symbolism of the rats, upon which no comment is made. Coming up to die, the rats are victims of the plague which besets the city. They are also perceived as, and certainly are, agents of the plague bringing death to the inhabitants. Finally, the plague exists independent of them, in *bacilli* borne by other carriers. Perhaps it is this aspect of Camus's symbolism which allows the critic to move swiftly from his drastic suggestion that the Algerian Muslims of 1955 have inherited a role previously assigned to their French masters and even to *their* (temporary) German masters. The silent beneficiaries of these interpretive flourishes would appear to be the opponents both of Algerian independence and French democracy – *les colons*. However this may be, the chapter on *The Fall* commences with a thorough summary of Camus's changing politics from 1944 until his death in 1960. Essentially, this follows the familiar pattern from post-war solidarity among the Resistance comrades, communist and non-communist, through a phase of 'principled' objection to 'political anti-communism', to an increasingly explicit right-of-centre position. In 1947 Camus

25

had recognized with horror that the French were doing in Madagascar and Algeria 'what we blamed the Germans for doing'. Ten years later his position had shifted drastically:

I have always condemned terror. I must also condemn a terrorism which operates blindly, in the streets of Algiers for example, and which one day may strike my mother or my family. I believe in justice but I will defend my mother before justice. (quoted p. 75)

The convolutions and evasions of Camus's position are not our main concern here, though it should be noted that this is the period immediately after the Hungarian uprising and the Suez crisis. Of greater concern to the more local battle of the books is Conor Cruise O'Brien's final evaluation of the author of *The Fall:*

Under its surface of irony, and occasional blasphemy, *La Chute* is profoundly Christian in its confessional form, in its imagery and above all in its pervasive message that it is only through the full recognition of our sinful nature that we can hope for grace. (p. 81)

So much may be taken as paraphrase, though hardly an unchallengeable paraphrase, of the novel. Far less uncommitted is Dr O'Brien's account of the emergence of the ironical *juge penitent,* a development in narrative method which

prepared the way for a different view of life, more conservative and more organic. Essentially Camus is beginning to take the side of his own tribe against the abstract entities. (p. 83)

There follows, to be sure, an expression of the feeling that Sartre may have been right and Camus wrong in their renowned political disagreement. But the study of Camus closes with a conjunction of Camus's 'tragedy' and 'Camus and his tribe', terms which bring us close to Yeats once again. The ultimate changelessness of change which Yeats epitomized in the revolution of beggar against beggar on horseback is bleaker than the posthumous world of the shades in 'Cuchulain Comforted', and it is to that world to which Dr O'Brien compares the 'faceless Arabs' of *The Outsider.* Perhaps Camus may be located among those purgatorial figures; perhaps indeed Dr O'Brien has kept the promise he made in his 1965 footnote: Yeats is redeemed of his fascism by Camus's movement from the Resistance to tacit approval of last-ditch colonial terrorism.

The Fontana Modern Masters book on Camus may take its concealed place in the recent growth of criticism in Ireland. Certainly, it has much to tell of its author as of its subject. The religious element in Camus's work – except when the Mediterranean solar myth is indulged – is accepted quietly, and so a futher link is forged between the author of *Maria Cross* and the eloquent radical of the late 1960s. Camus, for O'Brien, is clearly a highly charged subject: in ways which resemble each other (but never converge) each emerges from a divided, politically tense, background. Camus is a Frenchman in Algeria, whose pedigree is complicated by his mother's Spanish origins. In the suitably scaled-down proportion of things Irish, his critic is the son of a Catholic mother and agnostic father. Both mothers were widowed early, both sons had brilliant academic careers. These biographical parallels would be wholly unimportant were it not for the fact that, in his final assessment of *The Fall,* O'Brien sees Camus 'beginning to take the side of his own tribe'. This atavism, this rejection of socialism, has of course had its louder echo in Dr O'Brien's own political odyssey.

Virtually from the moment he took office as a Labour member of Liam Cosgrave's coalition government (1973), Conor Cruise O'Brien set about the rebuttal of any view of the Troubles which implicated a colonial or class basis to the conflict. His Labour colleagues had no difficulty abandoning class-analysis, but the denial of a colonial role played by Britain stirred up vestigial memories of the war of independence and before. As if to scotch any such memories, O'Brien went further, and argued that the Irish Constitution made, in effect, a colonial claim on the territory of Northern Ireland. From this it followed that the Protestants of that province, already hard pressed by the violence of the Provisional IRA, should be defended in all instances. Certainly, such an attitude appeared to be a classic case of putting one's tribe before all else. The problem lay in the knowledge that Dr Conor Cruise O'Brien was not of the tribe in question.

Some might see the validity of 'tribe' as a concept too easily conceded in so formulating the problem. It might be just possible to argue that, in defending the position of Ulster Protestants, O'Brien saw himself acting as the defender of secularism against the (at times) arrogant pretensions of the Irish Catholic hierarchy. It is difficult to see a secularist cause behind the condemnation (by a Presbyterian Moderator in 1986) of moves to allow shopping on Sunday as a 'Satanic assault'. In any case, as a minister and senator O'Brien was not distinguished in advancing secularist causes in the Republic; on the contrary, he made a number of gestures which seemed to suggest (or to confirm by way of gesture) that he was at heart a faithful follower of Mother Church, whose pontiff is annually condemned by Irish Presbyterians as the anti-Christ. The most renowned of these 'gestures' was an article in *The Observer* of 4 February 1979 under the title, 'Long Day's Journey into Prayer'. For the battle of the books the occasion is immaterial: what is highly relevant is the manner in which the idea of the tribe and its allegiances combines with a religious ideology most fully explored all those years ago in *Maria Cross*.

*'The self-same moment I could pray'*, so the article concludes. Admirers of the rational humanist did not abandon their hero: in Ireland gestures are not always precise signals. But earlier in the article O'Brien had explained how his own mother had returned to prayer:

My father had been agnostic. We lived in Dublin. Agnosticism ran in the family, a bit: my mother's eldest sister and her son Owen [Sheehy-Skeffington] were agnostic too. All the rest were Catholics, traditional, Tridentine. My mother had tried being agnostic, out of loyalty to my father. When he died she gave up and went back to being a Catholic. She also started to pray hard, very hard, even for an Irish Roman Catholic. She started praying on Christmas Night 1927. The reason why she started praying on that particular night was that my father died that morning, suddenly, of a heart attack, while bending a bow for me, my present from him.

You can forget about the bow. The important word, as any Roman Catholic sees instantly, is 'suddenly'.

This is not the moment for biographical excursion. On the other hand, the gravity of the cultural and political crisis we find ourselves in argues for some effort to understand our premier political critic. You cannot entirely forget the bow, I think, especially if you have read of Odysseus's return to

28

Penelope and the manner in which he proved his identity. In the context of 'Long Day's Journey into Prayer', the bow is strictly irrelevant – yet it is *there*. The two tribes of Irish politics have gathered round the bow, they are more especially two tribes in contrasting states of intellectual mobility, the agnostic/Protestant – I shall return to O'Brien's association of these two terms – and the soon-regenerate Catholic. The emblematic scene proves fatal for the first party, in contrast to the Homeric analogue, but proves spiritually revivifying for the second. Our question might be, how is it that Conor Cruise O'Brien some forty, fifty, and even sixty years later should devote his talents and energies to the defence of the first party?

If the answer lies as far back as *Maria Cross,* we should note before returning there the extent to which O'Brien's style has changed. Already, the tendency of his work to run off into a variety of impure forms has been noted – and no pejorative meaning is attached to this 'impurity' of form. It is as if the single, gathering current which might have issued as a series of magisterial studies had turned into a delta instead, the several streams of which actually flow away from each other, east and west. It is less easy to construct a benign metaphor for other aspects of his changing practice – the preference for newspaper 'columns' over more extended discussion, the proliferation of literary tags and name-dropping. (One *Observer* column drew on Burke, Baudelaire, I.A. Richards, Stendhal, and the 'Marat-Sade' play!)

*Maria Cross* dealt extensively with eight authors. As against the discrete gossip of the newspaper columns, the book has a discernible and intelligent focus. In a useful, if singularly ill-written pamphlet, Elizabeth Young-Bruehl and Robert Hogan identify this central concern of O'Brien's in his recurring concern with Claudel's play, *Tête d'or* and Mauriac's novel, *Le Désert de l'amour* – especially the character Maria Cross in the novel, who gives her name to the critical study. O'Brien summarized – having earlier elaborated – the essence of the play in the phrase 'Man remains nailed to his mother.' In relation to the novel, and as a final summary, he wrote of the 'community of pain, community in the acceptance of pain'. And went on to discover through the relationship of both a father and a son to the one woman (whose name *is* a female crucifix) that 'however much we may disclaim the tie, we are all related, like Raymond and his father – through Maria Cross' (p. 259). Here is the material for a definition of 'tribe' – albeit theological material – which might at once meet the violence of a 'community of pain' and inform the mysterious clarity of that community's *juge pénitent*. Here too, perhaps, is a source of the opposition encountered by any literary historian who seeks to work within social and historical categories.

# 3 Seamus Heaney's Preoccupations

THE WARM welcome given from the outset to Seamus Heaney's poetry suggests that he might be exempt from the controversies outlined here. The poems give such unalloyed pleasure to so many readers, the essays (collected in *Preoccupations*, 1980) display such respect towards a recognizable canon both Irish (Yeats, Kavanagh) and English (Wordsworth, Hopkins), that the press-ganging of their author into a troubled and uncertain critical argument appears heavy-handed. Yet the poet himself does nothing to confirm any complacency; his early pseudonym, *Incertus*, still has its propriety. Yeats was a poet many admired but – the record suggests – few positively liked. Seamus Heaney has overcome the rift between admiration and affection, while also managing to convey an unease at the ease with which both have come his way.

Between Thomas Kinsella (whose critical writing has been slight in bulk though weighty in implication) and Seamus Deane (whose criticism though not extensive tends to overshadow his work as a poet), Heaney stands in equilibrium. *Preoccupations* complements the half-dozen collections of verse, being substantial yet not academic, readable yet not trivial. The childhood landscape evoked in the opening essay is recognizably that of the early poems, and if the mythological sub-heading 'Omphalos' (p. 17) comes a little too pat, one should note also the manner in which ordinary rural sights and smells are converted in Heaney's account of them into something exotic, remote, accessible (the implication is) solely by means of some poetic gift. This may take us no further than the orthodoxies of Wordsworthian romanticism, and Heaney has indicated the extent to which the British school syllabus contributed to his early development. Late twentieth-century romanticism, of course, deserves courteous scrutiny, and it may be that there are affinities with American poets

(Theodore Roethke, A.R. Ammons) which deserve attention. In either case, or both, Heaney's poetic is distinctive in that his assumptions, romantic in shape and infused with a contemporary spirit, bear explicitly upon political and social questions. In this, Wordsworth may be closer than Roethke.

To judge by the epigraph he chose from a short essay of Yeats's published in *Samhain* (1905), Heaney has a particular sense of his title. The passage relates how the author of *Cathleen ni Houlihan* denied he had written to affect opinion; and, Yeats proceeds:

If we understand our own minds, and the things that are striving to utter themselves through our minds, we move others, not because we have understood or thought about those others, but because all life has the same root. Coventry Patmore has said, 'The end of art is peace,' and the following of art is little different from the following of religion in the intense preoccupation it demands. (p. 7)

This is Yeats at forty, Heaney's age as he compiled his *Preoccupations*. Impressed by the elder poet's high ambiguity in scarcely distinguishing between the 'following' of art and of religion, we risk missing how both poets have built Patmore's hopeless declaration more securely into position. Heaney's title enacts a further double reference. He is preoccupied with certain experiences, landscapes, writings, gifts: but one of these is the experience (landscape etc) of pre-occupation, of being where something other has earlier been and – in a sense – continues to be. Thus, he is concerned with Edmund Spenser as well as Robert Lowell, not least because Spenser was a previous occupier both of a physical territory and a poetic gift. 'The body' is a phrase held in common, surgery and archaeology, sexuality and injury are metaphors for a kind of exploration which is the essence of existence through poetry.

A poem where all these concerns come together employs the evidence of those human figures disinterred from the bog-land of northern Europe:

Here is the girl's head like an exhumed gourd.
Oval-faced, prune-skinned, prune-stones for teeth.
They unswaddled the wet fern of her hair
And made an exhibition of its coil,
Let the air at her leathery beauty.

Pash of tallow, perishable treasure:
Her broken nose is dark as a turf clod,
Her eyeholes blank as pools in the old workings.
Diodorus Siculus confessed
His gradual ease among the likes of this:
Murdered, forgotten, nameless, terrible
Beheaded girl, outstaring axe
And beatification, outstaring
What had begun to feel like reverence. (*North* p. 39)

The phenomenon of preservation by chemical process in the earth leads the poet immediately into a process of intense reflexivity. The girl's head *is* exhumed, and in the poem it is likened to an exhumed gourd. The beauty of her skin is leathery, though the material *is* leather. The absence of her eyes is compared to the pools from which she, now exhumed and exhibited, is absent. This palpable power of absence is linked explicitly to the manner of the girl's death: having been beheaded, she outstares the axe in the sense that she has outlasted it physically. In the final line she outstares, and also introduces, the poet's own response 'which had begun to feel like reverence'. It is only in these final words that the intense investment in a language conveying the empiric 'feel' of the exhumed figure relaxes to admit the (abashed) presence of the 'feeler'. He has been preceded by Diodorus Siculus whose ease also serves to introduce the theme of power (explicitly imperial power).

But if the title of Heaney's poem hints at Wilfred Owen's poem of a later imperial war ('Strange Meeting'), it echoes absolutely the title of Billie Holiday's song about a Southern States' lynching; echoes, repeats, appropriates the title as its own without making any reference to the local 'tribal' violence which is the song's material. (The song, 'Strange Fruit' was specially written for the singer and recorded by her in 1946.) With their disturbing undertones of eroticism, the twelve lines describe a 'pastoral scene of the gallant south/ the bulging eyes and the twisted mouth', but at no point admit an allusion, however slight, to any agent of this multiple slaughter and mutilation. Between archaeology, First World War poetry, and the American 'Blues', Heaney's poem searches for the silences and omissions which constitute his aesthetic bearing upon the violence of his native region.

It is hardly necessary to pursue this analysis with references to other poems from Heaney's canon. Nor is it necessary to spend much time in pointing to the political implications of such poetry written by an Ulsterman. Loss, disappearance, submergence; or, to be more exact, murder, death, sacrifice – these may be stages upon a course of preservation, preservation at a different ontological level. Heaney has never advised the Catholic community of Northern Ireland on the ethics of passive resistance, nor advocated a Masada-like last stand. Nor is he likely to do so. But the body of his poetry endorses a faith in the possibility that the tally of success and failure, which constitutes politics superficially, is inaccurate ultimately. Yet as soon as one has made that observation – adding that the elegies in *Field Work* impressively confirm the analysis – it becomes clear that Heaney does not share the confidence one might deduce from such a faith. He has not 'built' upon the growth evident in the successive collections of poems, but rather elaborated a kind of devout scepticism about such models of growth. The sequence 'Station Island' exploits the penitential exercises to great effect, though not without a little day-light poaching from *Four Quartets*. Emphatically, the twelve-part structure of the sequence refuses to adopt the fourteen-stage formula of the stations of the cross in traditional Catholic practice.

There is something in Heaney of that paradoxical Catholicism we found in Conor Cruise O'Brien's critical outlook, though the social determinants in each case are strikingly different. Neither could be described, adequately, as a conventional Catholic, yet their religious presuppositions are vitally important. The idea of sacrifice appeals to both, and it seems clear that Heaney is more aware of the dangerous egoism which can lie behind the idealism. In the critic's case, this Catholic inheritance has psychic as well as intellectual sources. In the poet's case, the politics of Northern Ireland provides an undeniable background of historic deprivation, prejudice, and petty victimization against which his imagery of sacramental loss defines itself. If the tribal divisions of that superficial politics are alluded to at all, it will be in tones of reluctant acknowledgement of the merely actual. Heaney is no radical, keen to bring the house down upon its sated proprietors. On the contrary, there is an unambiguous longing for accommodation with a social reality which, were it wholly ordinary, would be blesséd. This has led to the most bizarre appropriations of Heaney in the contemporary British educational system. Home being celebrated in a thoroughly bourgeois fashion, there has grown up a sentimental reading of his work whereby his evocation of that unattainable 'ordinary universe' is taken as an endorsement of the simulacrum on sale in the classier shopping malls. This attitude is attached particularly to the early poems; Heaney's later writing, while shifty as to political commitment, strives to render absolute historical amnesia relatively difficult.

*Preoccupations* reprints a piece about Lord Dunsany, in which he nimbly pin-points his subject's historical locus – 'Tory landlord. . . fantasist. . . typical titles. . . including, in 1934, *If I were Dictator!*' Not that Seamus Heaney is unyielding; half-quoting Yeats, he writes of Dunsany and his biographer:

There was some quarrel with himself which Mr Amory might have brought into focus, but, as it is, Dunsany emerges as a character who might be played to perfection by Terry-Thomas. . . (p. 204)

The Yeatsian willingness to discount the will, to regard the pursuit of art and of religion more or less as one, evidently has its attractions for the younger poet who nevertheless saw in the careers of John Berryman and Sylvia Plath the dismal as well as the divine aspects of that vocation. Against these, against their bravery, he acknowledges Robert Lowell as exemplary, and in an uncharacteristic moment of self-casting reveals how he and others considered Lowell's line 'my eyes have seen what my hand did' as an epigraph for Lowell's own tombstone. (This, note, in an essay called 'Yeats as an Example?') Lowell, for Heaney, was admirable because he 'held fast to conscience and pushed deliberately towards self-mastery' (p. 223). These pieces about Lord Dunsany and Robert Lowell are casual enough in themselves, but they contribute to the overall mosaic of Heaney's thought – Lowell, the Boston aristocrat turned Catholic, turned poet; Dunsany, the landowning fantasist; the one pushing towards self-mastery, the other a mere occupier.

Preoccupation, for Heaney, is not just a repetition of occupation, it summarizes an involuted reflexivity far more philosophically complex than its ostensive materials would suggest. His language has been praised for its exact reproduction of tactile experience, its ability to fuse reference and referent – for example, 'pash of tallow' where 'pash' enacts the soft snapping of the girl's brief candle and anticipates the transformation of sounds in 'perishable treasure' to suggest that it is 'perishable' which perished and a new treaure which is exhumed. Indeed, from exact reproduction to the fusing of reference and referent is but the first stage of a process in which the classic notions of metaphor and simile are put under enormous pressure, with tenor and vehicle collaborating and masquerading as each other. The poems 'Toome' and 'Broagh' come to relate to placenames rather than places, and the relationship between the human subject and his poetic place is progressively undermined in the opening of the first of these:

> My mouth holds round
> the soft blastings,
> *Toome, Toome,*
> as under the dislodged
>
> slab of the tongue
> I push into a souterrain
> prospecting what new
> in a hundred centuries'
>
> loam, flints, musket-balls,
> fragmented ware,
> torcs and fish-bones
> till I am sleeved in
>
> alluvial mud that shelves
> suddenly under
> bogwater and tributaries,
> and elvers tail my hair. (*Wintering Out* p. 26)

The conclusion of the poem at once rhythmically posits a surviving subject while also assimilating it into a wholly new

36

biological realm – these elvers, plural and active, are the 'living world' of the poem. In the companion poem, similar osmotic exchanges occur, this time not so much penetrating the distinction between subject and object as merging the senses in a single terminology:

> Riverbank, the long rigs
> ending in broad docken
> and a canopied pad
> down to the ford.
>
> The garden mould
> bruised easily, the shower
> gathering in your heelmark
> was the black O
>
> in *Broagh,*
> its low tattoo
> among the windy boortrees
> and the rhubarb-blades
>
> ended almost
> suddenly, like the last
> *gh* the strangers found
> difficult to manage.        (p. 27)

'Tattoo' is exploited as though it could simultaneously be the *visible* sign (a tattoo on the skin) and the *audible* musical drum-roll. Similarly, place is presented as an oral achievement in these poems, the enunciation of sounds which are infinitely refined, unique, beyond the ability of 'the strangers' whose attempts to manage the specific consonant they had visited are nicely cast in the perfect tense, 'found'. In these last lines some occupation, some mastery by strangers has been resisted (if not repulsed) by the language/landscape. Far from being a celebrant of local landscape, Heaney writes of landscape as itself something written, something ideally shared through a communal idiom, but as often elusive of enunciation. The community in question seems to be composed of ever-shifting subjectivities, with sometimes an excess of self and sometimes a deficiency being prominent. The two poems just examined are in this sense a pair – 'Toome' with its prodigal first person penetrating lavishly into a vocabulary at once sexual, geological and archaeological, only to find definition in the wholly altered intimidating last rhythm; and 'Broagh' passive, inert, revolving round the synaesthetic 'O' and the masterly copula 'was' to establish a *second* person singular ultimately adequate (?) to the plural strangers of the last lines.

It will already have struck the foreign reader of these poems, especially of *Wintering Out,* that they often alternate between allusions which are seemingly local and (to him) remote and a phrasing which is at once particular and abstract. In this, Heaney graphs, philologically as it were, the aesthetic restatement of the well-known principle of modern physics according to which the act of measuring falsifies the result of measuring. This is particularly apt in relation to subjectivity and the testimony of its fluidity in Irish society. The ego of a poem often sets off into a certain kind of engagement (cf. 'The Other Side', 'Casualty') and ends up altered: so much the average Dublin book-reviewer can comprehend, usually relying on the evidence of intractable social fact – sectarian difference, bereavement, etc – for an explanation. According to such readings, the poems are minor triumphs of learning on the poet's part. What both the foreign reader and the Dublin reviewer fail to appreciate is that Heaney's poetry involves a substantial philosophical difficulty in that this social evidence is ostentatious and uncertain – ostentatious because murder is a fairly rare topic for poems (even in America), and uncertain in that the poems are constantly on the point of allowing their own purely *symbolic* referentiality. Somewhere between the excess of self-consciousness and the inadequacy of existence, the Heaney ego puts one word in front of another and is by this alone changed, augmented or diminished. The bourgeois subject operates within a community by way of proportions rather than relations. The notable aspect of Heaney's poetry is that 'bourgeois subject' remains still a highly charged and historically problematic category in the social conjuncture from which he writes. Here too, resistance to any revision of our 'traditional' sociology has ironically landed Heaney in yet another job as laureate – this time, not of Habitat branches everywhere but of the Catholic tribes in south and west Ulster.

Kensington High Street and Aughnacloy *in uno*.

Of course, communal life in the poetry looms large, and the temptation exists to identify this preoccupation with politics *per se*. This would be a mistake. Community and politics are present in Irish literature as mutually exclusive opposites, Kinsella being perhaps the finest example of the writer who chooses the political option. There are undoubtedly moments in Kinsella's poetry where the communal and the domestic are evoked, but never in terms of longing, more often in the mode of that which absolutely has ceased to be, even though the light of that extinguished star (cf. Wordsworth's 'Michael') is still travelling towards us. Kinsella's dark searches in Gaelic proto-history, his readings of Jung and evocations of Mahler seem at first the very antithesis of the political option. However, the re-orientation of his oeuvre which commenced with 'Nightwalker' (1968) is essentially a political concern with the unprecedented de-politicization of a society increasingly given over to the tribal categories of Dr O'Brien and the ritual practices of Mr Heaney. The profoundly anti-revolutionary metaphysics of Heaney's poems stands in marked contrast to the implications of Kinsella's. That metaphysic comes very close at times to conceding a total hegemony to language, acknowledging its *imperium*, and to this extent the poet mimics the Sein-language of his admirers among the *Crane Bag* ideologues. We have yet to see what it is in the historical and social determinants of the Heaney canon which rescues him from that position.

# 4 Terence Brown and the Historians

IN 1965, the year before *Death of a Naturalist* appeared, Nicholas Mansergh published a new and revised edition of *The Irish Question*. This is the first, and arguably still the best, venture into Irish intellectual history, its chapter on the romanticism of Young Ireland being especially commendable. Mansergh was followed by many historians well able to accommodate literature in their reading of Irish history. L.M. Cullen's lengthy paper in *Studia Hibernica* (1969), 'The Hidden Ireland: Re-assessment of a Concept', undermined the picture of eighteenth-century Irish-speaking Munster advanced by Daniel Corkery in the original *Hidden Ireland* of 1924. Though less specifically literary in his concerns, Oliver MacDonagh has set about revising our ideas of relations between Ireland and the rest of the United Kingdom during the nineteenth century (in *Ireland: the Union and its Aftermath*, a book first published in the USA in 1968 but only really influential after the second edition appeared in Britain in 1977). The doyen of northern historians, J.C. Beckett, marked his retirement with *The Anglo-Irish Tradition* (1976); and F.S.L. Lyons, who (though younger) occupied a similar position in the south, published his Ford Lectures in 1979 under the Arnoldian title, *Culture and Anarchy in Ireland, 1890-1939*. At much the same time Lyons was appointed the official biographer of W.B. Yeats, following the resignation of Denis Donoghue.

All of this will suggest that Irish historians have been more confident in tackling literary problems than critics in acknowledging the difficulties bequeathed by their (older) historiography. The suggestion is largely true. Only Terence Brown has been able to match and – in the current stage of the race – outmatch the professional historians in laying the groundwork for an intelligent literary history. Brown's most important book, *Ireland, a Social and Cultural History, 1922-79*, first appeared in 1981, with a revised edition following in 1985. It can be shown, I believe, that the line of Brown's advance in the area of literary history – he began his career editing a book of essays on Louis MacNeice in 1974 – intersects with the historians proper at a time when their engagement with literature was being reconsidered and redirected. During the preparation of *Ireland, a Social and Cultural History* there had been signs of some slippage among the historians at the 'unhealthy intersection' (Conor Cruise O'Brien's phrase) of literature and contemporary politics.

Not enough attention has been paid to the specific politics shining through the pellucid pages of Provost Lyons's *Culture and Anarchy*. First, Lyons outlines the lengthy prelude to his chosen period. Then he proceeds to present the reader with the contrast between two cultures: an 'Anglo-Irish culture', itself distinct from the dominant English culture, and a 'Gaelic culture' with which some of the 'Anglo-Irish' attempted a fusion (p. 20). As the focus here is essentially nineteenth-century, should it not have been admitted that the 'Gaelic culture' to which the tyros of *The Dublin University Magazine* (1833-77) directed their gaze was essentially a thing of the past (the poetry in Hardiman's *Irish Minstrelsy,* etc), with its pastness ranking high among its attractions? Though the later revivalists of the Gaelic League (who included a few 'Anglo-Irish', like Douglas Hyde) doubtless thought themselves in touch with a still living reality, the results of their efforts might persuade us that pastness was what they sought for Gaelic culture also. Indeed, in passing, it is worth suggesting if the primary ideological function of the Gaelic movement was not to realize a contemporary redundancy, dance of death? We can distinguish two quite different usages of 'culture' in Lyons's argument here: the sense in 'Anglo-Irish culture' is essentially that of the anthropologists, i.e. it is constantly contemporary; while that involved in 'Gaelic culture' is profoundly archaeological, an antiquarian constant with a vestigial historical potential.

At the risk of awkwardness, I have stuck with inverted commas for several of these terms in order to prevent their becoming transparent and seemingly unproblematic. Citing Maurice Craig, Lyons himself concedes in a footnote that the term 'Anglo-Irish' may not stretch back any further than the 1840s, though elsewhere he uses it confidently to identify a whole 'culture'. But this dragooning of allegedly long-established social formations from latter-day coinages goes further when the conflict of cultures (there are three, we are told, in Ulster) becomes 'a war between two civilizations'. This latter phrase comes from Yeats (1903), though it was virtually anticipated by D.P. Moran (p. 61). Moran it was who coined the suggestively insecure tautology 'Irish Ireland', and moreover (Terence Brown elsewhere suggests) Moran it was who gave 'Anglo-Irish' its currency also. Precisely how one English-speaking, monogamous, carnivore Christian in Ulster differs from another in such fundamental ways as to constitute no less than *two* civilizations and as many as *three* cultures, we are not told (cf. the Inca, the Roman, the Assyrian). We are told, however, that this is 'a society none of whose cultures seemed to have a place for the urban proletariat' (p. 77).

Readers for whom the last-named body of men and women holds no terror may have begun to wonder if Provost Lyons has not been subtly rewriting Raymond Williams. If Williams tried to redeem something from Matthew Arnold in the title of his *Culture and Society*, Lyons has re-established the old antagonistic polarity. God knows the British Left has had little enough to say about the crisis in that part of the United Kingdom known as Northern Ireland, without its book-titles being appropriated. *Culture and Anarchy in Ireland* offers a view of Ireland not wholly at odds with the official British thinking of its day, though it also notes in passing the arrival across the island as a whole of 'the emerging Anglo-American culture'. (Has Williams infected Lyons's idiom just a little here?)

Though Lyons is concerned with the encounter of Catholic and Protestant in twentieth-century Ireland, he sets the defining clause of his argument in a nineteenth-century context, essentially that concerned with the emergence of various kinds of cultural nationalism. Oliver MacDonagh's *States of Mind* (1983) has a sub-title, 'A Study of Anglo-Irish Conflict 1780-1980', which indicates a time-span longer (at both ends) than Lyons's and a comparative attention to both of the islands. It is true that in the early pages comparisons of Ireland and Great

Britain are made, but these peter out as the notion of conflict becomes more active. Despite its individual merits, *States of Mind* exemplifies the slippage referred to above. Intent on cutting the posthumous reputation of Theobald Wolfe Tone down to size – an intention unobjectionable in itself – MacDonagh settles all too easily for a social categorization of convenience, arguing that Tone's middle-class origins placed him 'well outside the magic circle of the [Protestant] Ascendancy' (p. 73). This is a revealing focus of attack because it lends further credence – and at the hands of a distinguished historian – to the untenable sociology according to which the Protestant Ascendancy was a venerable and a veritably noble elite throughout the eighteenth century. Professor MacDonagh's acceptance of this (once) self-perpetuating notion is at one with his even odder timidity in the face of the *fact* that 'most Irish Protestants regarded religious and not secular allegiance as the primary principle of division in society' (p. 18). In his view, any gainsaying of this 'fact' by secularists or radicals constituted (both then and now) a 'dogma'. Thus one element in Irish society was licensed to mint the terminology by which all are to be identified, a state of affairs bearing a structural resemblance – at the least – to the latter-day Unionist veto. Writing of Tone, MacDonagh draws heavily on Tom Dunne, whose essay on Tone as 'outsider' [*sic*] uses Conor Cruise O'Brien's essay on Camus as source for a sociology of the Irish mid-eighteenth century. This, evidently, does not count as dogma. Not for nothing did one congratulate the Fontana Modern Master on taking his place in the first ranks of the present critical disputants.

*States of Mind* thus has its links with the less olympian historiography of *States of Ireland*. MacDonagh has no truck with loose talk about tribes, but his disinclination to question the coherence of Protestant Ascendancy as a social category allows the chance of establishing a firmer analysis of Irish society in cultural conflict to go by default. The disappearance of the comparative method promised in the sub-title is part and parcel of the same process of slippage. Conflict can be documented in relation to Ireland in 1848, 1865, 1916 – in relation to Great Britain it is not considered. Conflict *between* the two can hardly be denied, but the framework of the book (as it is rather than as it thinks of itself) ensures that the enquiry is focused almost exclusively on the western isle. In this we see the consequence of leaving unexamined the provenance of the term 'Anglo-Irish' which doubles up as an adjective qualifying relations between England (or Britain) and Ireland *and* as one qualifying certain relations within Ireland. MacDonagh's lively attention to the necrology of the Irish imagination in the 1860s (p. 101 etc) is not matched by any observation of the galvanic spasms, revenants, and other sundry ghouls who populate not only the English sensational novel of the day but also the sweeping lawns of Tennysonian verse. Both of these lost opportunities lead into the curious treatment of events after 1922 – a mere twenty pages concluding with an exposition of Seamus Heaney's 'Act of Union' as a poem which 'apostrophise[s] the price which Ireland pays for ancient British drives and current British absences of mind or will'.

If Heaney provides an alternative metaphor for MacDonagh's argument, *States of Mind* belatedly is taken up by another member of the *Field Day* team, Seamus Deane, as the vehicle for a further stage in the de-politicization of the battle of the books. It will strike Edna Longley as odd to regard Deane as an agent of depoliticization, but this ultimately is the altered direction of the *Field Day* enterprise. Anticipating somewhat, we can look briefly at Deane's review (in *The Irish Literary Supplement,* spring 1986) of MacDonagh's book. As ever, the piece is replete with passages of wonderfully intelligent summary and exposition, but it falters most revealingly on the issue of whether history gives access to a remediable social reality. Much of his response is cast in the interrogative mood:

I find myself asking if MacDonagh is. . . saying, this is how the facts have been (mis)represented and this is what the case really was and here is the reason for the kinds of (mis)representation we have – that being, primarily the colonial mentality which is itself the product of the Anglo-Irish relationship?. . . Can the report of any event be coincident with the event itself? Or is there an event itself? Historians rightly fear such nominalism; if accepted, it would make them mere writers, not scientists. (p. 39)

Not surprisingly, Deane concludes by hailing MacDonagh

'the historian as artist' who has 'given us all a lesson in how to read'. Deane's apparent willingness to step aside and admire the passing display of history – so different from Heaney's self-engendering, self-disturbing play upon the word 'exhibition' in the poem 'Strange Fruit' – comes as an abrupt acceleration of a tacit retreat from earlier ambitions. Like some suddenly cautious Whig of old, he finds in *States of Mind* the occasion to declare that 'somewhere along the line, interpretation has to run up against the ultimate; the labyrinth always has a centre, as well as a way in which is also a way out' (ibid.). This linguistic crane-baggage is untypically impenetrable in Deane, and the review is brief as – lamentably – all of Deane's writings are. Yet it is evident of the potent exchanges between the self-correcting work of the historians and the self-restricting inquiries of the critics.

Terence Brown thus inherits a sophisticated historiography which is visibly wavering in its ability to include the literary as conflict intensifies in Ulster. His need of this inheritance is conversely his reluctance to accept the available modes of specifically literary analysis. In an early book, *Northern Voices: Poets from Ulster* (1975) he had dourly observed that

the degree to which the young poets of the 1960s received local approbation and the patronage of an enlivened [northern] Arts Council has tended to cloud the fact that their work has been, in the main, stylistically conservative and thematically unsurprising. (p. 172)

In the later *Social and Cultural History* he concentrates on exposing the comprehensive nature of this conservative legacy. At the Last Judgment, or in a perfect society, Brown's history may come in for some criticism – it is largely dependent on secondary sources, and pays just a curiously minimal attention to the sub-state of Northern Ireland under devolved rule. In the absence of these apocalyptic tribunals, his work is simply the very best available.

The fourth chapter deals with the fate of minorities, and these turn out to be two in number. The Irish Left may be an intellectual – and indeed political – minority, but its social constitution is that urban proletariat F.S.L. Lyons saw unaccommodated in Ireland's cultures. Brown's treatment concentrates on the weakness of the Irish Labour Party after independence, and this despite its association with the radical and internationalist perspectives of James Connolly (1868-1916):

The cultural effects of this socialist eclipse in twentieth-century Ireland are not far to seek. The socialist ideas and preoccupations of much of modern Europe have curiously little currency in a country where ideology has meant protracted, repetitive debates on the national question with, up to very recently, little attention directed to class issues and social conditions. Indeed, one of the obvious weaknesses of Irish intellectual life in much of the period has been the absence of a coherent, scientific study of society of the kind that in many European countries has its roots in a socialist concern to comprehend the ills of a manifestly unjust social order. (p. 105)

The origins of this weakness clearly lie further back than the generation of the Provisional IRA, with their brutal substitution of sectarian violence for political development, a substitution in no sense mitigated by a 'food-parcel' provision of advice centres for one of the sects concerned. They lie further back than the eclipse of the Labour Party in post-Treaty Ireland. They must be sought at least in the last quarter of the nineteenth century when, by contrast, a highly articulate, reflective and active intelligentzia in Europe provided a critique of High Culture itself. The subsequent sociological study of culture, whether Marxist (in Lukács, Korsch, Benjamin etc.) or non-Marxist (Weber, Durkheim, Mannheim), provided a base for the scientific study of the interaction of religion and economics, class and culture, regional and metropolitan forces. The absence of any such critique in the Irish context is felt daily, like an amputation.

One aspect of this situation in particular deserves a further moment's thought. The contrast with Europe is a persistent resemblance (both real and imagined) to Britain. This is no less true of independent Ireland than of the old days of the United Kingdom of Great Britain and Ireland. The difference between the two islands in this exclusion of scientific, philosophically grounded sociology might be expressed as a debit and credit, the profits accruing in an easterly direction. Instead of such a sociology, British intellectual life pioneered the anthropology of primitive cultures, and repaid the material debt by elevating the most underdeveloped regions of Ireland to the heady role of culture-fodder for Modernism: Yeats's west of Ireland in league with Frazer's anthropology.

Brown declines to trace the Left any farther off-centre than the Irish Labour Party, missing an opportunity (for example) to re-assess the Republican Congress of the 1930s and *its* failure. Treatment of his second minority provides him with an admirable base from which to correct the post-socialist revisionism of Conor Cruise O'Brien. This second minority is the Protestant population of the Irish Free State. Brown's choice of minorities echoes O'Brien's association of agnostic and Protestant, but is more explicit in relating his material to the operations of institutional Catholicism within the new political structures of the Irish state, the sense of insecurity and hyper-caution which followed independence, and the intellectual feeble-mindedness of these minorities themselves. Though willing to acknowledge O'Brien's need to direct attention away from the old ideology of aggressive nationalism while in office, Brown insists on identifying 'what was intellectually depressing about the revisionism' of this period:

Implicit through Cruise O'Brien's writings in the 1970s was the suggestion that Ireland would have achieved as much as it did had the Easter Rising not taken place, had that 'unhealthy intersection' between literature and politics not been fabricated. A mind capable of severity and astringency on other matters became markedly self-indulgent on this issue.

In short, Brown laments the 'unhistorical quality' (p. 290) of O'Brien's thought in this area, and proceeds to analyze the fate of the southern Protestants with a less dramatic sense of tribal *Götterdammerung*. The persistent role of Protestant families in key areas of economic life is noted, together with their impressive (and generously state-subsidized) educational advantages. It would be sentimental to suggest that Terence Brown, born (albeit in China) of Protestant, clerical stock, is innately better equipped for the task of analyzing relations between class and creed in Ireland than Dr O'Brien with his ecumenical background and socialist credentials.

# 5  *The Crane Bag* (1977–1985)

EIGHT YEARS after its foundation *The Crane Bag* was taken into voluntary liquidation by its editors, Mark Patrick Hederman and Richard Kearney. This was not the result of financial disaster or editorial disagreement. On the contrary, the magazine had spectacularly solved many of the problems which had bedevilled *Atlantis* a decade earlier. Distribution was good, publicity was good, and there was an endless supply of material. Why then should a successful magazine close down? What is the larger significance of *The Crane Bag's* demise? How does it interact with the rift between historians and critics?

One area where it differed from its predecessors was the exclusion of creative literature. The reasons for this have never been clear. Irish critics, philosophers and ideologues are a pretty fractious lot, but compared to the poets and novelists they exude harmony and good will to all persons. A magazine rid of trouble-making literature might be expected to have a longer life, just as a man cured of a toxic addiction might outstrip the biblical span. On the other hand, magazines are intended to create a certain kind of trouble, and *The Crane Bag* was not in other respects averse to stirring things up. It did not neglect the visual arts, it commented extensively on philosophy, it shunned history apart from isolated panoramas of County Meath, it attended conscientiously to events in the Third World. But it excluded literature as such. This did not prevent Mark Patrick Hederman from devoting a last editorial to 'the possibility that art is the most potent guide to the riddle of what it means to be fully human in the last quarter of the twentieth century. . .' This possibility leads to

an inner journey through the labyrinth of the poet's own history and situation to a point of release onto the open space of otherness. It is not a physical journey, either to the west of Ireland or Europe. The geographical

48

place may well be a point of access, just as we can reach the ubiquitous [!] world of an underground railway by walking through the portals [!] of any and every local or provincial station. The 'exile' of the poet is symbolical and always represents, paradoxically, a 'homecoming', because the journey he undertakes is one whereby he comes into his own ground, where he reaches 'the first circle' of himself. (vol 9 no 1, pp. 112-113)

Heidegger and Dale Carnegie may have the rest of the day off.

Although the point was never made explicitly, it seems that the editors privately held the view that the dominance of literature over other kinds of cultural enterprise constituted the very problem they wished to tackle. It is a view which deserves further discussion. Instead, special issues became the special feature of *The Crane Bag*. Mythology, the images of Irish women, the northern question, 'a sense of nation', the Irish language, mass media and popular culture – all these were specialized topics which yet possessed a degree of general appeal. Apart from the loyal following that any successful journal develops (and in Ireland it is small), *The Crane Bag* addressed itself to a number of atomized audiences rather than to the public as such. The special issue on minorities (vol 5 no 1, 1981) amply illustrated the point: so many interest groups, class fractions, cliques, bands of walking wounded, were attended to that only the majority of the Irish population escaped. This is not to express some moral majority opinion outraged by the privileges granted to Irish-speaking Unionist sculptors: it is rather intended as an indicator of the profound sense of uncertainty underlying the frenetic energy of *The Crane Bag* editors. Conversely, it indicates a qualitative change in the structure and behaviour of 'the Irish public', a change the journal responded to but could not adequately analyze.

The Ireland perceived was a parlous confederation of vulnerabilities. The magazine set out to chart these psychic areas, to identify their principal features, to advance some general pathology explaining how things came to be as they were. But no routes from area to area were mapped. The team employed on the task was huge, as befitted an exercise in intellectual field-work comparable to the Ordnance Survey of the last century. The final issue, for example, gave a platform to no less than thirty-seven contributors who dissected 'Irish

49

ideologies'. Dissect is not perhaps the most accurate word, for the discussion more resembled a pre-operative consultation with interns, medical tyros and a few urbane specialists all pursuing their signifiers up their signified. The printed interview, with all its inbuilt opportunities for repetition, pointless gesture and inconclusiveness, was a format much favoured in *The Crane Bag*. Looking over the complete file, one is undoubtedly impressed by what it achieved in introducing new ideas into the Irish debate on politics and culture generally, less impressed by the impact of those ideas themselves. Richard Kearney was unique among the large group of Irish theorists in making a formal submission to the New Ireland Forum.

I am well aware that this account of *The Crane Bag* has leaned heavily on the mixed metaphor, and the dependence is neither wholly accidental nor wholly without significance. Despite Kearney's formidable mastery of contemporary French theory, and the distaste of that school for eclecticism, the magazine he edited displayed a pluralism of approach going beyond generosity to begin to resemble hesitancy. Or caution. The *Irish Times* of 11 December 1985 carried an obituary for the magazine which indicated that moves towards a more tightly ordered intellectual outlook had led to a loss of patronage and, hence, to the abandonment of the entire project. Kearney is quoted as saying that

It is symptomatic of the Irish intellectual tradition to confine philosophy to the consideration of literature. The original concept of the *Crane Bag* invited an open debate between art and politics, but sponsors and the Arts Council began to look askance when we began turning our attention away from strictly literary matters.

Moreover, the *Irish Times* reporter notes that the special issues on Latin America and 'Socialism & Culture' brought readership to a low level, while the issue on Northern Ireland cost the editors a grant. The apartheid between politics and the philosophy of culture was not broken down, and every comparative exercise was resisted by the public. So rather than contribute to that apartheid by changing intellectual course, the magazine closed. Besides, the editors were tired.

There were times when the contributions were tired also. The issue on Northern Ireland did not produce any new insight or propose any new course of action. (There were *four* interviews.) Conor Cruise O'Brien's contribution to the 'Minorities' issue was marked by the re-emergence of that most exhausted argument allegedly comparing North and South – the condition of the Protestant minority in the Irish Republic. Dealing in the tribalist terms we now see as characteristic of his categorizations, Dr O'Brien is enabled to show that Ulster Protestants see their southern brethren 'as having, in effect, ceased to exist as a distinct community, through the twin effects of the emigration of the intransigent, and the absorbtion of the acquiescent' (vol 5 no 1, 1981, p. 47). This argument rather neatly avoids the observation that emigration from southern Ireland was for long an experience affecting every social group, the causes being simple economic hardship and lack of opportunities both material and intellectual for growth. (The Left, Terence Brown's other significant minority, arguably lost a great deal more through emigration – Jim Larkin, Jim Gralton, Sean O'Casey, not to mention all those nameless and named Irish activists in the socialist movements of Scotland and England.)

The silent dismissal of the facts of social history in favour of a tribal theory of eviction, sacrifice and so forth is not of course unique to Dr O'Brien. Even within the highly restricted area he selects, the statistics hardly bear out the predetermined theory. In my own family, many have emigrated in this century from what is now the twenty-six county (*de facto*) republic – perhaps fifty people in all. Only two have travelled northwards to Ulster; one by way of marriage prior to 1916, the other by way of a dozen years in Africa, arriving in Fermanagh in the mid-sixties. It should be remembered that the majority of southern Protestants are middle class or lower middle class, that they have signally refused to identify with the northern state of affairs, and that their difficulties (with differences of course) have been shared with their Catholic neighbours. For every burnt-out Big House emblematic of Anglo-Irish alienation from the new realities of the Free State, there is a score of Methodist salesmen, Church of Ireland middling farmers and Presbyterian businessmen, who decline to become statistics in Dr O'Brien's tribal calculus. Nor did the fleeing masters

51

of those burnt-out Big Houses show much preference for life in Sir James Craig's province when it came to choosing an alternative domicile. Most went to metropolitan life in England, not simply because it was England but because it was also metropolitan. Some went to Africa (South, and east), where late opportunities for lording it over the natives still persisted. In the case of some, there was the simple logic of accredited imperial servants heading for the mother country – stool-pigeons returning to roost, a refreshingly vulgar image offered here and now to re-orient our view of the captains and the kings. In how many cases can one show that even these loyalists anticipated Dr O'Brien's admiration for not-an-inch Ulster? Certainly not in Sir Edward Carson's, as the founder of Ulster Unionism, born a Dubliner, died an embittered man in England. What, finally, of the other statistics, those showing the migration of frightened Northern Catholics southwards?

Though O'Brien's contributions were hardly typical of *The Crane Bag,* they had a place in its logic, its indiscriminate eclecticism. His impressive double-bill appearance as prophet of doom and escapologist, rubbing the reader's nose in unsavoury but intractable realities (the murderous nature of the Provos) while keeping his own unpolluted by any acknowledgement of SAS and UVF activities, facilitated some of the more pompous formulations of the *Crane Bag* programme. Thus, in the editorial already quoted, Mark Partick Hederman expanded on his notion of 'the fifth province'. Long, long ago, some people thought that the four provinces of Ireland 'met at the Stone of Divisions on the Hill of Uisneach' thus positioning a fifth not unlike Euclid's definition of a point: 'others say that the fifth province was Meath (Mide), "the middle" though they disagree about the location. . .' (vol 9 no. 1, p.47). Anyway, 'the purpose of *The Crane Bag* is to promote the excavation of such unactualized spaces within the reader, which is the work of constituting the fifth province'. One hopes that Head-gardener Heidegger was able to return to his equally timeless task of legitimizing tribalism – 'only the *Fuehrer* himself is German reality and its law' (*Freiburger Studentenzeitung,* 3 November 1933, translated).

# 6 Having a Field Day

IN ITS theatrical aspect, the *Field Day* company is part of a revival of provincial-based drama, a movement which has also seen the emergence of the *Belltable* theatre in Limerick, the *Druid* in Galway, and the *Hawkswell* in Sligo. In a positive sense, Derry and not Dublin is *Field Day's* base, even though most of the directors live outside Northern Ireland. Brian Friel's *Translations* (1981) and Thomas Kilroy's *Double Cross* (1986) indicate as much in their names as in their historical material a concern with dualities of identity as experienced in the Irish past. Between these two plays, the company has been much concerned with modern adaption – of Greek myth by Tom Paulin, and Molière by Derek Mahon – a further dimension of translating and crossing over. As we shall see, this latter renovative preference is in keeping with the broader priorities of the pamphlets which constitute the company's explicit contribution to critical debate.

I have already touched on the central role of the project in the critical skirmishes of the 1980s. It is time to look in more detail at these nine pamphlets. But, first, some more intimate views of the participants themselves. Brian Friel is the senior partner; photographs tend to show him seated, in semi-profile with his face turning towards the camera; he appears confidently secure in his approach to the world. Seamus Heaney is the best known, a friendly yet hurt expression gently containing the violence he knows as his material, his inheritance. Tom Paulin's shoulders are hunched forward, though whether in assertion or defence it is hard to say; the expression is pained but humorously borne, as befits a front-of-the-house man. Seamus Deane is usually depicted standing, the dark pullover hinting at a confident deviation from the strict clerical garb which might have been his two generations ago. David Hammond is more often heard than seen, the folk singer *par excel-*

*lence:* a voice in which purity and experience movingly converge. Stephen Rea: though he is the only partner who lives professionally in the public eye, is less well known; as an actor he is also recognized with something of a pleasant shock. Rea, Hammond and Friel have not written pamphlets. Paulin and Heaney have written one each, Heaney's a verse-letter. Seamus Deane has written two. Pamphlets nos 5-9 were the work of outsiders to the group, one of these being Terence Brown whom we have already met.

It will not be necessary to comment on each at equal length, but a tabulation of titles and authors may be helpful.

1983  1. *A New Look at the Language Question*, by Tom Paulin.
2. *An Open Letter*, by Seamus Heaney.
3. *Civilians and Barbarians*, by Seamus Deane.
1984  4. *Heroic Styles: the Tradition of an Idea*, by Seamus Deane.
5. *Myth and Motherland*, by Richard Kearney.
6. *Anglo-Irish Attitudes*, by Declan Kiberd.
1985  7. *The Whole Protestant Community: the Making of an Historical Myth*, by Terence Brown.
8. *Watchmen in Sion: the Protestant Idea of Liberty*, by Marianne Elliott.
9. *Liberty and Authority in Ireland*, by R. L. McCartney.

This neat list of three titles per year disguises some salient features of the operation. First there comes a solid concentration of perspectives provided by the central members of the team. Then there is a gradual relaxation of this exclusive discipline, to include Declan Kiberd whose contribution fits fairly comfortably into the established idiom, and Richard Kearney (allied through *The Crane Bag*) who takes the *Field Day* interest in myth to new areas of contemporary experience. Finally, when the debate has been set up in terms which readers recognize as *Field Day's,* three more thoroughly external contributors are admitted, one of these (Robert McCartney) being a practising Unionist politician. While it is unlikely that the gradual relaxation of editorial control was in part the result of adverse criticism – *Field Day* was characterized by one leading novelist as 'three men praising each other' – it should also

54

be recognized that the more paranoid hostility of some commentators was based on a premature assumption that exclusivity was the project's unalterable policy.

Nevertheless there have been shifts of ground within the central argument, as Edna Longley has noted. The most obvious has been the attempt to give a voice to certain kinds of Protestant anxiety or to a historical perspective on that anxiety. The polar tension between history and myth remains central; it has long been a favourite preoccupation of Deane's, and may be traced also in his contributions to *The Crane Bag*. While the pamphlet series is still young (and one hopes it will continue to expand), a number of missing topics must be listed. These include (a) the Irish language as cultural totem in the nationalist view of things, and as irritant in the Unionist view; (b) the role of the Catholic Church in political and social life north and south of the border; (c) the whole question of social class as an alternative to denomination in describing society; (d) the population explosion in the South, especially of the urban young; (e) nuclear energy, neutrality and US/ British defence interests in Ireland. The core of these (as yet) unattended issues is the nature, existence and future viability of the nation-state.

Despite these omissions, it is undoubtedly true that *Field Day* has set the terms for the current debate in Irish criticism. Other positions have to be seen as reaction against, or specialized applications of, arguments brought forward in the pamphlets or in other company projects. A 'narrative' of the pamphlet project to date can now be sketched. The first three publications are much concerned with language. Paulin compares the implications lying behind the lexicographical practice of Samuel Johnson, Noah Webster and James Murray. Though he seizes on the susceptibilities affected in the 'British/ English' distinction, he leans heavily on the idea of nationality and national pride as motivating factors in the production of language. In conclusion, he argues for a dictionary of Hiberno-English (or Anglo-Irish), in the course of which argument Ulster loyalist research into a distinctive linguistic past is accommodated. Seamus Heaney rejects the label 'British' as applied to him by the editors of the *Penguin Book of Contempor-*

*ary British Poetry,* but admits that the resentment is tardy, a kind of *esprit d'escalier* (p. 7):

> it's like the third wish,
> The crucial test.

Though Heaney considers ancient history and eastern European politics, the real shape of his argument is revealed when the above-quoted magic formula leads on to a vision of Ulster's ravishment, giving birth to the terrible twins (p. 11):

> One a Provo, one a para
> One Law and Order, One Terror –

That binary pairing recurs in Deane's first pamphlet, where a denunciation of civilized law as self-authorized force leaves itself open to the interpretation that it virtually sanctions the bomber outside the law. (This is one of the vulnerably ambigious positions from which Deane's more recent writings may be regarded as a defensive regrouping.) Writing under the lingering influence of the hunger strikes, he finally concludes that 'political languages fade far more slowly than literary languages but when they do, they herald a deep structural alteration in the attitudes which sustain a crisis' (p. 14). It is precisely at this point that one is first disappointed by *Field Day's* neglect of the state as the primary political concept in crisis.

The second triad is more concerned with literature. In his second contribution Deane takes up Paulin's interests to posit (temporarily?) that 'Irish writing [in English] is dominated by the notion of vitality restored. . . This is one of the liberating effects of nationalism. . .' On the same page (p. 7) he points forward to Kearney's contribution, writing 'the revolutionary tradition [that Patrick Pearse] represents is not broken by oppression but renewed by it'. Kearney duly takes up the theme, equipped as a philosopher of religion, and contrasts *mythos* and *logos,* the latter glossed as rational critique. He proceeds to see the 'sacrificial martyrdom' of the hunger strikers as an episode in mythic process. (He does not, here at least, advert to Francis Shaw's useful and half-suppressed *Studies* paper on the proper theological definition of martyrdom.) The Social and Democratic Labour Party manifests a 'piety/

secularity' polarity, while in the area of literary history there is. . . yes, a Yeats/Joyce polarity. After some shuffling, Kearney comes down on the side of *mythos* rather than rational critique, it seems to me, though remaining alert to the duplicity innate in the former. Declan Kiberd is more secular. Ireland and England are his juggling toys, Wilde and Shaw the jugglers. Kiberd is strongly against the antithesis whereby people make 'absolute divisions not just between English and Irish, but also between men and women, good and evil. . .' (p.7). His characterization of Ulster Protestantism as 'barbarous vulgarity and boot-faced sobriety' (p.22) belies this incipient dialectic.

The third triad is concerned with religious history, contemporary history in the case of the ninth pamphlet by Robert McCartney. More significantly, this section of the developing project is also narrated by outsiders. These later pamphlets are longer than the initial ones, commencing with Terence Brown's searching inquiry into the Victorian origin of some current beliefs held of and by Ulster Presbyterians. Though not fully self-contained it augurs exceptionally well, in its break-down of the alleged homogeneity of 'the whole Protestant community', for his more extended book on nineteenth-century Irish literary history (due from the Skellig Press in 1988). Robert McCartney is more concerned with individual liberty as conceded and denied (to various degrees) in the Irish Republic today. He analyzes the proceedings of the 1984 New Ireland Forum, especially the contributions of the Catholic hierarchy. Marianne Elliott, in what is arguably the finest performance in the whole series, draws out the co-existence of radicalism and anti-Catholicism in 1790s' political theory, and stresses the Irish Protestant preference for a strict legalism of the word even when conflict with a sponsoring authority in England resulted. All three pamphlets bear witness to the essential contradiction of Presbyterian politics: the emphasis on democratic forms *within* the presbytery, and the dismissal of any notion of those outside as having a countable franchise which might constitute a valid majority. The Presbyterian Church's report, presented in advance of its 1986 deliberations, serenely assumes Northern Ireland as a whole to be

57

such a presbytery, and the authority of the British government to speak merely for such a non-valid majority. Among reviews of this third series, *Fortnight's* (9 September 1985) by the Revd Terence McCaughey deserves especial attention, written as it is by one who is himself a Presbyterian minister who reveres the radical tradition. McCaughey makes a point insufficiently stressed by the three contributors, that Irish Presbyterianism had *two* kinds of radicalism: in addition to the radical conservatism which foundered on the proposition to give Catholics representation in parliament, there was the progressive strain of Jemmy Hope and others who emphasized 'the relations between the classes'.

The larger narrative of *Field Day* can now be appreciated. Commencing with a consideration of language as a synchronic system disengaged from history (though occasionally decorated with window displays of antique emblems), the pamphlets have finally engaged with history, albeit a history strictly tied to sectarian topics. The need for this change of direction – it is only one, the traffic heads in both directions – was perhaps detectable from the start in recurrent, isolated, yet potent allusions to Edmund Spenser, for it is with the Elizabethan period that the crucial history begins. While awaiting the intrusion of historical reality, the series devoted itself to a sequence of essentially binary propositions concerning region/centre, demotic/standard (idiom), Irish/British (national identity), civilians/barbarians. In the second phase the discussion reached back to the nineteenth century, but no further, and the binary propositions took on greater coherence and precision in the comparisons of Wilde and Shaw, Yeats and Joyce, myth and history. Though the culmination of the process takes place in the work of non-company contributors, there is a counter-flow in which the discussion of literature and its relation to politics is actually returning towards the centre of the field, returning indeed to formulations not wholly irreconcilable to the critical vocabulary of pre-*Field Day* critics. Despite an air of iconoclasm and innovation, the company's principal achievement to date will turn out to be a reformulation for the late twentieth century of an aesthetic already implicit in Yeats. Reformulation, of course, necessitates renovation at least, and certainly goes beyond veneration and recitation, but the revolutionary consequences of Seamus Deane's initiative may soon appear strictly limited.

One indication of this unconscious, postponed conservatism may be found in *Field Day*'s indifference to literary experiment, another in its tendency to regard the literary present as considerably longer than the political present. Declan Kiberd (admittedly not an official member of the team) addressed an American conference on Irish literature's lamentable preoccupation with the past, and used Yeats's *Deirdre* (of 1907!) as his example. Moreover, as Edna Longley has pointed out in reviewing Deane's *Celtic Revivals,* the neglect of that 'intermediate generation' of Austin Clarke, Frank O'Connor, Sean O'Faolain and Flann O'Brien (and, one might add, of Jack Yeats, Joseph O'Neill and Brian Coffey) jeopardizes the emergence of a convincing literary history (*Irish Literary Supplement,* fall 1985). Of course, Deane has subsequently published *A Short History of Irish Literature* (1986) which to some degree cancels Ms Longley's complaint. But the neglect of experimental modernism in O'Brien, experimental Thomism in Coffey, sustained social critique in Clarke and Jack Yeats – these remain serious omissions of the *Field Day* programme itself. Deane has very usefully drawn attention to the work of at least two neglected Irish novelists – Eimar O'Duffy (1893-1935) and Gerald O'Donovan (1871-1942). Even then, the literary preoccupations of *Field Day* have an odd shape, with one emphasis lying in the immediately pre-independence period and the other in a period roughly coterminous with the members' own active lives. Officially de-constructing nationalism, they effectively by-pass the classic phase of the Irish State as a stable political entity.

The political present, on the other hand, defines itself fairly neatly, and largely in terms of the northern conflict with its all too evident sectarian lines of division. The traditional Irish aesthetic, which continuously implicated politics, is being reformulated in terms which will suit a Northern Ireland stabilized round the permanence of Provo and Loyalist intransigence. This will pose no great problem for an economy increasingly geared to 'high mobility investment'. In the light of these developments, silence on the topics of state and class becomes understandable, to say the least. The erosion of sovereignty has been a matter of public knowledge ever since the debates on joining the EEC. As for class, the traditional recourse to history has, if anything, only served further to confuse and obscure the origins of Irish class formulations and the (different but related) origins of an Irish class terminology. Post-industrial Irish society, based on an economy of atomized process in ever-changing and accelerated programmes of plant closure and worker 're-education', can easily accommodate itself in the tribal compounds of a sectarian sociology. Of course, talk of post-industrial society will irk some commentators who feel they have yet to reap the benefits of classic industrialization, but the term serves to suggest that the kind of political unconscious of which Fredric Jameson has written may be traceable below, and in stark contrast to, the manifestos of *Field Day*.

Such judgments may be premature, and *Field Day* has concrete achievements which deserve acknowledgment and applause. Whether innovatory or renovatory, radical conservative or radical progressive, the company has lifted Irish critical debate to a new level of informedness, of stringent openness. Though there are survivors from the era of Blather-about-Beauty and Books-for-the-Boys, rampant anti-intellectualism is less possible in debate now than it was twenty years ago. More indebted to the brand of French structuralism which in migrating to the USA lost its political edge, Irish criticism even at its most embattled has a robust good humour. Here, it resembles *American* political criticism (cf. Jameson, Said, Watkins, Owens, Johnsen) rather than the sanctimonious factionalism of the British New Left. At the risk of lending more creditability to that respectable sprite 'the autonomous bourgeois individual' than my credit allows, I should still pay tribute to Seamus Heaney's deep human kindness, to the warm intelligence everywhere evident in Seamus Deane's writing, and – not least – to Tom Paulin's buoyant pessimism.

# 7 Edna Longley and the Reaction from Ulster: Fighting or Writing?

THE MOST persistent critic of the *Field Day* enterprise has been Edna Longley. Southern-born and educated, with a background including Catholic as well as Protestant relatives, Ms Longley has taught for many years in Queen's University, Belfast. A distinguished critic and editor of the work of Edward Thomas, she is immensely popular with her students (especially women) and occupies an unrivaled place in the academic profession in Ulster. Her sustained opposition to *Field Day* has thus brought the new propagandists directly into confrontation with the view of literature obtaining in the universities. In one sense this is ironic, as Ms Longley's education at Trinity College, Dublin, can hardly have inculated anything more-up-to-date than the practices of the Georgians – her conservative stance is more advanced than that of her origins. In another sense, however, the critical method she adopts seeks to act as a defence not only of literary works exposed to a new onslaught from partisan ideologues but as a defence of the Northern Irish 'state' itself. The fallacy of her position is not so much one of critical theory as of political fact – Northern Ireland is not a state.

The Belfast-based review *Fortnight* has been her principal platform from which she has addressed the issues in question. In addition, she has edited (with Gerald Dawe) a collection of essays in honour of John Hewitt, *Across a Roaring Hill: the Protestant Imagination in Modern Ireland* (1985). (A further book of essays solely by Edna Longley is imminent.) Her case against Seamus Deane and his colleagues is not wholly consistent, but it has undoubtedly concentrated issues in the public mind, and stimulated a degree of splenetic response (especially from Declan Kiberd). A review of Tom Paulin's collection of poems, *The Liberty Tree,* in the summer 1983 issue of *Fortnight*

61

(no. 196) may provide a helpful starting-point.

Edna Longley here discusses the work of three authors, Derek Mahon, David Rudkin and Paulin himself. 'Mahon's poetry's poetry deeply absorbs the failings of his people', whereas Rudkin's play, *Across the Water,* takes 'blood-guilt into ludicrous realms of sado-macochistic fantasy'. One cannot quarrel with her comparative evaluation of Mahon and Rudkin, and can enthusiastically echo her suggestion that – the pointlessness of models notwithstanding – Mahon is a model in his 'ever more difficult relation to his own culture intensified by absence'. No, the quarrel arises when one comes to measure exactly how substantial and how distinctly exact that 'culture' of Mahon's (putatively) may be. It is in such criticism that we see the results of F.S.L. Lyons's slippery usage in *Culture and Anarchy*. The problem with Lyons is not so much his emphasis on *difference* between various population groups in Ulster, it is his total silence on the massive degree to which they share a common pattern of behaviour and assumption, including a common belief in their difference. It would be a thoroughly and crudely reductive reader of Mahon's poetry who would see it as primarily concerned with, and valuable as, Ulster Protestantism. Ms Longley is not, generally speaking, a reader remotely of that kind: she is unlikely to see William Faulkner simply as a Confederate white or Samuel Beckett as a Dublin bourgeois. Her political categories, however, persuade her of the temporary advantages of seeing Mahon in this way, partly because it provides a stick with which to beat (the conveniently masochistic) Rudkin, and partly because it is a stage on the way towards buttressing the notion of Mahon's *people,* the Protestants of Ulster. The reasons for this second manoeuvre will become evident in a moment. For the present we note that, with Mahon as her prism, the light of Protestantism is discernible as 'failings' which can be absorbed, whereas 'blood-guilt' is now a stigma borne by Rudkin rather than his people. Indeed Rudkin is effectively expelled by this gentlest of parliamentary suspensions. Before he goes he provides a system of reference by which Tom Paulin's figures (Sol Grout, or the Revd Bungo Buller) are seen as 'caricature colonialists' and 'satirists' negatives'. It might be worth Ms Longley's pondering that need of blood-guilty Rudkin to come to terms at all with Paulin's poetry. To dismiss a helicopter in Paulin's poem simply 'as seen on Channel 4' is to miss an opportunity to consider the apparatus of Ulster violence as televised entertainment, and the anaesthesia thus induced. The conventional frontiers of Edna Longley's criticism, its satisfaction with the perimeters of print and a one-way system of allusion, are evident here.

The major case against *Field Day* is made in her review of the second series of pamphlets in the July/August 1984 issue of *Fortnight*. The title of Ms Longley's piece, 'More Martyrs to Abstraction', while it may not have been of her choosing, negatively underlines the commitment to the organic/concrete as a desideratum both in literature and in the discussion of it. It may be pointless to suggest that a critical vocabulary devoid of abstractions – like 'critical' and 'vocabulary' perhaps? – is an impossibility for everyone except Swift's Flappers. Nevertheless, it is important to show how Edna Longley's assumptions have their specific loyalties to British empiricism with its valorization of the individual and his/her 'experience'. Deane's offence, in her eyes, is as much that he argues from a position which attributes to social entities the energy and 'creativity' which the conventional critic arrogates to the individual imagination. The tendency of such critics to merge the individual and the work is rarely more evident than when Longley summarizes Deane's attitude to Yeats: 'Deconstruction reduces "many ingenious things" to rubble.' Deane is a weekend deconstructionist who would not get a union card from Paul de Man or Harold Bloom, and Longley is not really in doubt about this. The term 'deconstruction' is useful to her as a rhetorical weapon whereby she establishes his seeming hostility to Yeats whose poems become (in her rhetoric) the lovely things they allude to. Deane's real offence is that he stands outside these assumed intimacies. When he argues that the superiority of a poem by Yeats over one by Patrick Pearse is 'finally defensible only on the grounds of style', she is misled into missing the unexceptional ordinariness of the judgment, believing instead that Deane is labouring to remove the distinction between literature and life! One cannot avoid the suspicion that Pearse's metrical foot in the door is resisted because of his suspect politics. It is reasonable of Ms Longley to suggest that *Field Day* puts itself 'in line with static Nationalist views of history', but there is a note of desperation in the follow-up which speaks of 'the incurably absolutist thought-processes of even sophisticated Nationalists'. Dealing with the threatened arrival of Pearse on the scene, her writing shifts between these alternative tonalities:

[Deane's] false separation between form and content indicates the risks run by literary critics when they dilute their obligation to the totality of a text, conscript texts for propaganda. They produce literal-minded, single-minded readings which respect the fine print of neither poetry nor politics.

One might be forgiven in mistaking this for an off-the-record rebuke by György Lukács to some less dialectically refined comrade, but of course Edna Longley does not use totality as Lukács does, as a mediation between 'form' and 'content'. Her point might have been clearer had she simply referred to the *integrity* of the printed text on the page, and complained of Deane's Lukácsian tendency to go behind the mere 'fine print'. By standing outside the assumed intimacy of text-as-reader, Deane renders conspicuous everything the practical critic sedulously excludes from view. Since 1920 Northern-based critics have done little to establish a 'totality' which relates the pentameter and outdoor relief riots, pastoralism and the B-Special constabulary. There has been no active equivalent to Yeats's strictures on southern society, or those of Sean O'Faolain, Hubert Butler and Peadar O'Donnell in *The Bell*. It is reassuring therefore to find that Longley's last sentence in this review is an endorsing transcription of 'one sentence of Deane's [which] renders most of his others unnecessary':

The acceptance of a particular style of Catholic or Protestant attitudes or behaviour, married to a dream of a final restoration of vitality to a decayed cause or community, is a contribution to the possibility of civil war. (see *Heroic Styles* p. 16)

But then it is the previous isolation of Northern critics from social life which has made Deane's case both inevitable and unpalatable. The quotation from Deane continues from where she leaves off, 'it is impossible to do without ideas of a tradition. . .'

The sub-title of *Across a Roaring Hill* refers to the 'Protestant Imagination in Modern Ireland'. In this collection of essays, Longley, as co-editor with Gerald Dawe, sought to establish the dignity and substance of an element in Irish culture which she evidently felt had been discounted in recent exchanges. It still seems to me, after months of thought and discussion, a calamitious error of judgment to have constructed the collection on what can only be regarded as an exclusivist Protestant franchise. Here again is that collusion of subject and object which we saw in her defence of Yeats against what was deemed Deane's deconstruction. Yet the crucial feature of *Across a Roaring Hill* is not its team of contributors, but its exclusions. Imagination is quietly assumed to be exclusively a literary faculty. Music, painting, sculpture count for nothing: nothing on Brian Boydell, Frederick May or Elizabeth Maconchy; nothing on Jack Yeats (so powerful a contrast to the highly defended elder brother), or Louis Le Brocquy or Cecil King; nothing on Oisin Kelly. There is even very little on theatre: nothing on Wilde, Shaw, Augusta Gregory, O'Casey, the Longfords or Denis Johnston. (Wilde, you may think was Victorian, but he was a good deal more modern than Forrest Reid for all that Reid's escapism might tell us about the separation of politics and aesthetics in the Unionist north.) Once the Abbey was bereft of Yeats, it might have seemed that it stood in Catholic (as nationalist) contrast to the more cosmopolitan Gate under Edward Pakenham. One has only to recall the background of Lennox Robinson, F.R. Higgins and Earnan de Bladh to see this neat sectarian schema dissolve before the eyes. This neglect of the theatre, like the wholescale exclusion of the non-verbal arts, can only be explained by reference to the inoperancy of the Catholic/Protestant schema in these areas. 'Words alone', it seems, 'are certain good' when it comes to constructing a sectarian sociology of art. If Seamus Deane had erred in deconstructing Yeats, more than adequate compensation has been paid: in *Across a Roaring Hill* the very boundaries of criticism are set according to the precept of line ten of the first poem in the *Collected Poems*.

It is worth pausing to consider this extraordinary politics

of the word. The empirical tradition relies on a notion of the self which is wholly outmoded in philosophical and scientific terms. There is a distinct group of Irish writers, a group including Samuel Beckett, Louis MacNeice, Flann O'Brien, Elizabeth Bowen and Francis Stuart, in whose very different *oeuvres* the whole metaphysics of identity, the self and so forth, is subject to an intensely sceptical scrutiny. The group locates itself round the date 1939, for behind the interrogation of the idea of the self lies a broader involvement in the issue of Ireland's identity and integrity *vis-à-vis* Europe at war. MacNeice catches a central preoccupation in *Autumn Journal* (II): 'Who am I – or I – to demand oblivion?' This concern with the possibilities of self-betrayal is an urgent instance of a larger crux: the sense that writing poetry (Yeats's 'words alone') necessitates, at a conceptual level, a Self-betrayal with its libidinous potential and potential for emancipation. Abjuring the abstraction inherent in painting and music, avoiding the dialogism and activity of theatre, *Across a Roaring Hill* longs for an embodiment of the imagination in the self. One has only to look at the poetry of Derek Mahon, who is a next-of-kin to many of the Group of '39, to see such longings subjected to another sceptical scrutiny. The whole ambition may of course be declared hopeless, and nobody knew this better than Yeats who interested himself nevertheless in the racial theories of S.J. Stuart-Glennie, Nazi eugenics and other matters. Race and Self are totems in creeds which long for an exclusive claim on reality. If Yeats never suscribed unreservedly to such simple-minded notions, he nonetheless borrowed odd back-numbers from the circulating library of racial ideas. The conjunction in some northern criticism of a sectarian sociology and a 'hands-off' attitude towards Yeats is revealing. Over two hundred years ago George Berkeley noted:

One great Cause of Miscarriage in Men's affairs is that they too much regard the Present. . . But the Grand Mistake is that we know not what we mean by we or selves or mind etc. (*Philosophical Commentaries* 839, 847)

The defence of the Self, of the integral text, is inevitably a political apology for the present.

My own contribution to *Across a Roaring Hill* covered some of these points, but more particularly argued that there is a line of descent from the anti-revolutionary rhetoric of Protestant Ascendancy in the 1790s to the intermittent fascist leanings of Yeats and the never-fully-articulated racial exclusivism behind Unionism. This line of descent is made more difficult to delimit (and hence to resist) by the absence of any figure like Thomas Mann whose critical decoding of his own heritage is such a conspicuous element in the German resistance to fascism. (There is now some evidence of this examination of conscience beginning in Irish Methodism, starting some years ago in the work of Eric Gallagher and breaking into print in David Hempton's *Methodism and Politics in British Politics 1750-1850* (1984).) This theme did not elicit any response from Declan Kiberd who, in reviewing the *Roaring Hill* twice, continued to demonstrate the preponderant appeal of sectarian rather than socialist categories. A refusal to acknowledge even the existence of an argument concerning the emergence of a sectarian sociology in the 1790s leads promptly into a capitulation in the face of that ideology. Thus, 'a true Irish intellectual is both Catholic and Protestant', and most of the Literary Revivalists sought 'a fusion of two cultures and two religious traditions', all of which finely discerned literary history leads us to the proposition that 'Beckett's habit of stopping his play to remind us that it is a play is a slow-motion re-enactment of the puritan closure of the theatres' (*Fortnight,* 21 October 1985).

Recently Ms Longley has been joined in her battle with *Field Day* by John Wilson Foster, now a resident of the Canadian Pacific coast. Dr Foster's initial contribution to the debate was an early one, *Forces and Themes in Ulster Fiction* having appeared in 1974. At the time it was generally regarded as a pioneering study, especially in its attention to such neglected early-twentieth-century novelists as Shan F. Bullock. This regional definition had its negative side of course, omitting consideration of those writers who did not satisfy a somewhat crude definition of regionalism. Thus, 'Ulster fiction' was elaborated without any reference to Flann O'Brien (unquestionably the most complex novelist to come from any quarter of Ulster) or to Francis Stuart (the most politically *engagé* novelist with an Ulster background). Excluding O'Brien's experimental modernism, and Stuart's various migrations across ideological frontiers, British/German, Protestant/Catholic, haut bourgeois/bohemian, republican/loyalist etc., it was not difficult for *Forces and Themes* to represent Ulster fiction as realistically concerned with the mystique of region and the perennial antagonism of denominational loyalties. Virtual silence on Patrick Kavanagh's fiction indicated another implicit assumption: that a southern orientation in the post-partition period disqualified even so regional a novel as *Tarry Flynn*. In retrospect it is easy to see that Foster's Ulster is essentially that forged by the Home Rule crisis of 1912-14: territorially, that is the six counties remaining in the United Kingdom, plus Donegal for summer holidays.

Since 1974 Foster has published a large number of articles, some of which take up this relationship between culture and topography. In this way his criticism links up with the work of Estyn Evans, whose vast contribution to historical geography accommodates a rationale for the post-partition boundaries of the new Ulster, legitimizing its 'stand-off' from the rest of the island. Foster rejoined the debate at a conference in Tacoma (Washington) with a paper subsequently delivered in revised form to the Belfast meeting of the International Association for the Study of Anglo-Irish Literature – both meetings in 1985. The text has been published in *The Honest Ulsterman* (no. 79, autumn 1985) under the title 'The Critical Condition of Ulster'. The opening sentences run:

The critical condition of Ireland at the present time seems undivorceable from the condition of criticism in Ireland. The failure of Irish society is the failure of criticism.

If there is a tinge here of what Sam McAughtry calls 'yo-yo writing', one should not be distracted from observing how an energetic application of structuralist notions deriving variously from Lévi-Strauss, Roland Barthes (in their politically inert versions), the later ideas of Jacques Derrida and Paul de Man, leads to a triumphant return by the great Victorian liberal imperialist, Matthew Arnold, with all his old nostrums for the impractical Celt. But the best part of Foster's analysis is devoted to elaborating and rendering the several contradictions he sees in the *Field Day* pamphlets, and here he is at his most acute as a critic of critical texts. Indeed, Edna Longley's unfailing condemnation of structuralist 'jargon' has been winningly muted and transmuted by Foster's playfulness in tying the ends of each *Field Day* contradiction together so as to immobilize its implications. Having decided that Seamus Deane's second pamphlet reveals him in the process of abandoning a nationalist redoubt, Foster urges all and sundry to 'maintain a critical discourse in wilful neglect of hereditary or acquired political discourse'. More simply '"Culture, not politics" ought to be one of our slogans.' The yo-yo could not be in or out of better hands.

Foster shares Longley's illusion that Northern Ireland is a state, and indulges notions of a 'democratic majority' there. This congruence of the infra- and extra-presbytery is not likely to reassure those of a different denomination. But, in the end, he is more concerned to make a stand for a sort of perverted class-perspective. With a characteristically ebullient flourish, he opines:

the autonomous individual may be a bourgeois humanist fantasy, but many of us in Ireland would like to enjoy that fantasy, thank you very much. . . it would be foolish for us to embrace the psychological socialism of post-structuralism before reaping the rewards of psychological *embourgeoisement*.

'Us', of course, has been defined by 'the claims of sect and heritage [which] will remain and remain legitimately, helping as they do to form this explanatary self' of bourgeois humanism. On foot of this warrant, the terms of Seamus Deane's parole are posted: liberated from the despotism of fact, he is to be permitted 'a series of public seminars up and down the country'. But lest Deane should think of writing any 'political prescription' into these seminars, Dr Foster neatly discredits the presence of any such thing in one pocket by hypothesizing 'a gun in the other' pocket. Having long forgotten the admission two minutes ago of Irish society's *failure,* he now recommends 'the existing order of things till right is ready', an Arnoldian programme from which no B-Special would have seceded. Ulster as autonomous text.

While Jack Foster was making his way from academic immiseration on the Pacific coast to the prospects of *embourgeoisement* in some future Ulster, Edna Longley returned to the fray, reviewing *Field Day* pamphlets 7-9 in *The Honest Ulsterman* (no. 79, autumn 1985). Having earlier accused Seamus Deane of abolishing the last distinction between life and literature, she opens with an odd overview of the first two series of pamphlets, seeing them

shaped by grievances of the Irish writer/academic, not by the forces that truly affect people's lives. Hence the attack on Yeats: a much more visible figure in the study, than to either Irish society or English politicians today.

What these 'forces that truly affect people's lives' are, Longley declines to tell us at any length. She is downright in charging Robert McCartney with glossing over his own party's dismal record on liberal legislation, yet proceeds in the next paragraph to credit him with clearly perceiving 'nationalism's desired package-deal'. The reasons given for his clear sight are more impressive than any account of nationalist wickedness; McCartney, it seems, 'belongs to a threatened species'. If we take the fine print of this seriously, we find that the adjective 'threatened' has done away with any thought of tracking down details of the wicked package deal, while the insinuation of genocide by means of 'species' (however you huff and puff) more than stands in for the elusive details. The forces that truly affect people's lives include a sense of racial or (in the strictest philological sense) *special* identity.

At the New Irish Forum of 1983/4, Seamus Mallon of the SDLP elicited a significant response from the Church of Ireland delegation. Mallon wanted a description of the real hopes and fears of the 'ordinary Protestant/Unionist', and he was answered by Lieutenant Colonel Filor. The colonel declined to rely on the old slogans or invoke the Union Jack and Sunday observance, but concluded nonetheless that 'those are all symptoms, outward signs, of an inward deep feeling *which I do not think can be expressed in words*' (emphasis added). With its odd echoing of the catechismal definition of sacraments, this can hardly increase one's trust in rational debate. Refusing to articulate its position, Unionism renders it unassailable, a strategy wholly consistent with the politics of the word enacted in *Across a Roaring Hill*.

70

Of course, since the Forum, London has shown an interest in an *additional* position, additional in that the Hillsborough Agreement nowhere abandons the unique guarantee to the Ulster Unionist minority that the state's integrity is their monopoly. Yet the shock of Hillsborough has driven Unionists to claim 'alienation', previously a condition denounced as a Marxist buzz-word in Catholic pastorals. One literary critic felt a need to declare his true blue loyalism in the letters column of the *Belfast Telegraph.*

Colonel Filor's merging of the pathological and the sacramental, symptoms and inward grace, as an expression of the inexpressible unwittingly unveils a nexus of projected guilt and transcendental security. Such thinking is difficult terrain for critics, and the various strategies of northern poets with Protestant antecedents – Derek Mahon and Michael Longley being the most notable – seek to overcome this valorized inarticulacy, and yet also to minimize (whether by pastiche or by the cultivation of more strictly domestic *lares et penates)* this overblown degenerate metaphysic. Paradox abounds – for example, Colonel Filor's ineffable concert with the sonic boom of instantly redundant phrases, and Harold McCusker's declaration in a radio interview that Unionists could never 'work their salvation' under the Hillsborough Accord. It is just this confusion of salvation and security which authorizes today the substitution of sect for class, and inscribes the apocalyptic binary divisions of Judgment Day upon housing allocations in County Fermanagh.

# 8 Waiting for the End (or a Beginning?)

*Why does the history of the Orient look like a history of religions?* Marx to Engels, 2 July 1853

*It's not the despair, I can stand the despair, Laura. It's the hope.* Brian Timpson

FORTUNATELY, the debate is not quite finished. The other battle has not yet taken over, though there are significant banks of silence building up on the intellectual skyline. Failure to discover a means of propagating a coherent, perhaps even a scientific, socialist critique of culture in Ireland has been documented in a variety of instances, personal and otherwise. Instead, the crucial years since 1965 have seen an exponential growth of introductions, summaries and short histories of Irish literature, all of which avoid any deeper, more sustained, more hazardous inquiry. Literature has thus become heat-resistant, packaged in ways very similar to those of the supermarket: A Modest Proposal Without Tears, Grants for Goldsmith, Plumtree's Potted Myth. It is isolated from the other arts, and is in danger of being jilted by History, its most attentive (if at times chauvinistic) lover. Finally, its critics have been systematically denied any sociological rigour in the simple description of class society. Literature *is* the Irish ideology. This state of affairs places on the writer a particular responsibility to the reflexive relations which necessarily link his/her art to social reality.

I want to conclude this contribution to an unconcluded debate by drawing attention to two instances of repression in the ideological area. The first of these has a blatantly personal basis, and concerns the reception of my own book, *Ascendancy and Tradition in Anglo-Irish Literary History from 1789 to 1939* (1985). I hope that the preceding pages have given some indication of the importance for the present crisis of earlier failures to define the terminology of Irish cultural debate, and of the even greater importance of the 1790s as the forcing ground of certain crucial elements in the terminology. The second is far more remote and impersonal: the attitude of the British 'literary left' to the crisis in that part of the United Kingdom which they sometimes recall under the name Northern Ireland. In order to avoid any sense of conclusive judgment, the remainder of the argument will be locally sub-headed.

## i. 'Ascendancy – shows belief in astrology' (Synge)

From the dates of its sub-title, *Ascendancy and Tradition* does not appear to have any bearing on our current discontents. My first concern had been to clarify some of the social categories existing throughout this period (1789-1939) of Irish literary history, from the French Revolution to the outbreak of the Second World War. More particularly, I concentrated on the origins of Protestant Ascendancy (a new concept in the process of valorization as ideological badge) in debates among the guild members of Dublin Corporation and in the Irish House of Commons early in 1792. These origins were urban, bourgeois and commercial. To produce a dozen witnesses to this less than Augustan provenance for Protestant Ascendancy was to challenge the version of history steadily advanced by W.B. Yeats and passively adopted by most of his critics. It also threatened to undermine a well-established sectarian sociology by making clearly traceable in class terms that 'false consciousness' which is the basis for innovations like Protestant Ascendancy that, in a twinkle, are venerable and traditional.

Given the thorough-going imposition on the Ulster crisis of an apocalyptic concentrate of that ideology, any demythologizing of Protestant Ascendancy to reveal its monopolist and middle-class origins in anti-revolutionary alarm would have run into trouble. For a start, it tended to undermine the claims of latter-day Ascendants to protection from the alleged tyranny of London and Dublin, a tendency commensurate with the extent to which these latter-day Ascendants are seen (by themselves and others) as the misfor-

73

tunate remains of a once noble caste dragged down by English Whiggery, Jesuitism and Peter Barry. There can be, however, no guarantee of a counterbalancing hurrah from their opponents, in whom moral consolations for victimization have been carefully inculcated over a lengthy period to produce – most recently – the Pyrrhic election of Seamus Mallon to Westminster.

Anything which bothers all of the parties to a particular row is denounced by them as eclectic, each finding too much of his antagonist's material turning up side by side with his own liturgical incantations. Though Augustine Martin (*Irish Times* 8 February 1986) gave the book his qualified and yet generous imprimatur, he was visibly disturbed by the variety of critical approaches he uncovered. Criticism, it seems, is at its best when it anticipates the immaculate and single-minded integrity it would ascribe to the work of art, or when it happily resolves the balance of tensions it happily approves. A criticism which either strives to draw in and render explicit the contradictions operative in its own permitted sphere of operation, or which employs a variety of strategies within a totalizing philosophy, will be dubbed eclectic by the most metaphysical of eclecticists.

Denis Donoghue, writing in the *TLS* (1 November 1985), has some pertinent complaints about the treatment of Yeats's 'Nineteen Hundred and Nineteen', though the merging of several chapters in his summary of one (non-existent) chapter does not instantly recommend this kind of close reading. Professor Donoghue's real complaints are devoted to the demythologizing of Protestant Ascendancy:

My own view [he writes], which nothing in McCormack's book has persuaded me to abandon, is that only the phrase 'Protestant Ascendancy' was conceived in 1792, when it is first recorded as having been used. Under several other designations, such as 'the Protestant interest', Burke's 'the new English interest' or, in R.B. McDowell's phrase, 'the Protestant Nation', the social formation was firmly in position as soon as William won the Boyne. In 1840 T.D. Gregg justly referred to 'the old Protestants who made ascendancy their rallying cry in the time of William the Third'.

There is certainly much to chew on here, not all of it food for thought. On the basis of a mass of evidence he declines to cite, Professor Donoghue concludes that the phrase 'Protestant

Ascendancy' was first conceived and first recorded in 1792. (My own statement of the case was more cautious.) After two further sentences, he has agreed with the Revd Tresham Dames Gregg that it had been the rallying cry of the Williamites! This seventeenth-century rallying cry has now been recorded twice, once by a mid-Victorian demogogue, once by a New York professor in 1985. As against these recording angels of 1690s' war cries, others might consider evidence from the 1790s of Protestant Ascendancy's being then a new ideological element – the evidence of Edmund Burke, Henry Grattan, George Ogle, William Drennan, Wolfe Tone, William Ogilvie, *et al*. The characteristic of *this* school of reviewing is the neglect of argument and evidence in favour of tradition.

To be fair, Donoghue counters philosophically that all this is evidence only of a new phrase, nothing more. Such a notion of the relationship between language and non-language is surprising in one whose work has been noted for its blend of philosophical and literary facility. Surely we are not invited to accept that Interest=Nation? That would be a use of language unworthy of the reviewer. And Protestant=new English? That would be a 'use' of history worthy of the IRA. If 'the Protestant Nation' is Dr McDowell's phrase – which I greatly doubt – then, the man I heard lecturing wonderfully last November must be at least two hundred years old to have provided a *prior* designation of the Protestant Ascendancy! One cannot but be impressed by the intellectual sacrifices reviewers of this school are prepared to make in the name of consistency with the past.

The issue of dating Protestant Ascendancy correctly is directly concerned in the debates of the present, where the resultant sectarian sociology plays such a prominent role. The emergence of Protestant Ascendancy in 1792 did not leave things unchanged, cannot simply have been a lexical visitation from nowhere without influence anywhere. The verbal collocation had in fact occurred some five years earlier in a pamphlet controversy, and if these instances modify the statement in *Ascendancy and Tradition* that January 1792 is the earliest date at which it has been discovered, the argument concerning its emergence in the political arena still stands. The near-simultaneous transition from 'Catholic Relief' to 'Catholic Emancipation' is a related case of new terms carrying (being propelled by) an increased emotive force. Such intensification contributes a further factor to the developing sectarian sociology of the nineteenth century. The accretion of *early* eighteenth-century associations, together with a rural, landed and quasi-aristocratic hinterland, is not under way until well into the nineteenth century, and crucially not until the 1840s and after. These developments have immense implications in any reading of the historical background to the present crisis in Ulster. Moreover, a coherent literary history needs an analysis of class somewhat more sophisticated than that offered by the Revd Gregg.

*Ascendancy and Tradition* being as much historical as literary in its concerns, a *TLS* reviewer has need to deal with its historical thesis. Singling out a reference to 'the gradual erosion of landed estate as a political reality during the nineteenth century' he speculates:

What can he mean? According to W.E. Vaughan's *Landlords and Tenants in Ireland 1848-1904* (1984), in the 1870s 20% of the country was owned by landlords with estates ranging from 2,000 to 5,000 acres, and over half the country was owned by less than a thousand great landlords. Between 1847 and 1880, 90,000 evictions were recorded, 50,000 of them in the period 1847-50. In 1861, 203,422 people were admitted to workhouses. The Land War of 1879-82 can't be shrugged off.

At first sight this looks like the real thing, and a sign from heaven that an Irish literary critic has been vouchsafed an historical view from Pisgah. But there are immediate problems, statistical, logical and historical. The reviewer's source is a fifty-page pamphlet, and not the magisterial authority he allows it to appear. However, it is a very fine pamphlet and having provided a statistic of 90,000 *recorded* evictions, it proceeds to instance one notable case:

[Vaughan writes] The biggest eviction ever recorded by the police took place on the estates of Trinity College, Dublin, in 1851 when, according to the police, 753 families were evicted in Kerry. The Board of Trinity College has often been accused of oppression, but there is evidence that on this occasion the Board was innocent and that the evictions never took place. [He then advances three independent sources of evidence.]

76

It seems that in this, as in the definition of agrarian crime, the RIC had attitudes to evidence and to statistical methods of their own. But where has this taken the *TLS* reviewer in challenging the remark about the gradual erosion of landed estate *as a political reality*? Implying that I shrug off the Land War of 1879-82 (which the landlords certainly did not win in any triumphal manner), he cites a statistic for evictions in 1847-80, more than 55% of which occurred in the first three years of that period – the period being, it is highly significant, immediately post-famine. If Trinity College is not wholly unconnected with the late eighteenth-century emergence of Protestant Ascendancy ideology, it nonetheless fails to fit the bill as an individual herditary tyrant. And if Dr Vaughan is right in his contention that the particular College evictions never took place, there is solid evidence of other corporate bodies evicting tenants from their Irish estates. Unlike the College, the Law Life Assurance Society of London cannot be easily absorbed into that blur of prejudice which has found 'the Protestant Ascendancy' an admirable deputy for a proper analysis. Of course the operation of limited liability companies as 'landlords' in the post-famine period is not at odds with the essentially bourgeois and mercantile provenance suggested for Protestant Ascendancy. But it is less exciting for reviewers of the school of impenetrable truth.

The very late Victorian and Edwardian society which is the starting point to *Field Day's* literary present is masked in Protestant Ascendancy, just as the growth of recreational landlords – the Wildes, the Bewleys, for example – in Connemara actually underlined the extent to which the middle classes had penetrated that 'feudalism' Michael Davitt so unhelpfully observed in late nineteenth-century Ireland. Those obtrusive inverted commas indicate how thoroughly conventional language enfolds particular historical interpretations – the personalizing of ownership in land*lords* even when ownership had developed into far more complex structures, and an insistence on the ancient basis of a rural society more thoroughly overturned, altered and renovated than any other in the British Isles. Such masking assists Professor Donoghue in failing to distinguish between legal power to evict and political power (of the kind which might have made the Land War turn out the way he curiously thinks it did). Finally, there are two disparate remarks of his which should be brought together. In the review in question, he remarks, 'it is no longer respectable to propose a typology of races'. Elsewhere, post-scripting the *Field Day* pamphlets, he announces:

The man to beat is Yeats. . . But while an argument can be refuted, and a thesis undermined, a vision can only be answered by another one. I don't think that any historian's evidence would make any difference to Yeats's vision, or dislodge it from our minds.

Thus, finally, the impenetrable truth.

## ii. *New Left Review*

If the premier critic of the iconographic school has settled for a mere assertion of his marvellous dismissal of Coleridge's 'suspension of disbelief', it might be thought that the angry young persons of the British New Left were immune to such failings. This is not the occasion to look back on the odd coyness of English critics, from Leavis to Eagleton, in the matter of twentieth-century Irish writing: let us take a more concentrated and less personal sample, the files of the *New Left Review* itself. Founded in 1960, it has published over one hundred and fifty issues in twenty-six years, during which period Northern Ireland has thrown up the single most sustained challenge to the 'normalcy' of British politics since the 1790s. Being generous in my counting, I find perhaps ten articles during that quarter-century which relate, in some loose sense, to the Irish crisis. This figure includes a selection of Paul Hogarth cartoons, three articles by Conor Cruise O'Brien (between 1965 and 1967), a review of a biography of Feargus O'Connor, and two pieces by Tom Nairn on the break-up of Britain. The cover of issue no. 55 (1969) bore the helpful legend, 'Explosion in Ulster', and the review's coverage of that detonating moment consisted in two interviews and an article by Peter Gibbon, No. 43 (1967) had the German and English text of a poem by Yaak karsunke [*sic*] entitled 'Kilroy was Here'. karsunke's poem was not the most negligible of *NLR* treatments of Ireland. Compared to that record, Denis Donoghue is a model of attentive responsibility.

The present situation is extremely depressing and distressing for anyone at all concerned with the problem of reading contemporary literature in the processes of social life. The Left claims a particular talent in this regard, but in the Republic of Ireland the Left has been immobilized since the start of the civil war. In the United Kingdom, however, there has been a sophisticated and voluble socialist movement engaged in the most abstruse inquiries concerning literature and society, ideology and reality: the only question seemingly neglected is the one upon which the state names itself – the inclusion of Northern Ireland. From 1966 onwards that disputed area has been central also in the renewal of poetry (in particular) as a component in educational and cultural administration. But the New Left says nowt.

Instead, the sectarian divisions of Ulster society are taken as normative and permanent. Not only does such passivity underwrite the suppression of any analysis in terms of class, of exploitation by rapidly changing forms of industry and capital, of the place of Ireland in the Western defence system; it also encourages, urges, indeed compels (as we have seen even in the case of so fine a critic as Edna Longley) the reduction of literature to the status of authenticating evidence on behalf of one tribe or the other. The poem *as such* very rarely evinces even a potential to become a reflective and critical element in the network of relationships which constitutes its reception: for the most part, it is taken as either lyrically affirmative or tragically satirical, or as an exhibition of temporary ecumenism arranged between these two doctrines.

## iii. Field Day Revisited

It begins to appear that the sharp exchanges in Irish criticism over the last two decades or so have been both more and less than ancestral voices prophesying 'an unacceptable level of violence'. *Less,* in that the combatants can be shown to have much in common, do not represent opposite corners of any significant philosophical arena. *More,* in that their disputes and exchanges actually constitute the acceptable level at which violence and repression may be decoded – the sectarian or tribal level. *Field Day* initially gave the appearance of pitting history against myth, but the implicit preference for history has not been sustained or, where it has been endorsed, the task has been contracted out to others. Seamus Deane's lecture, 'Yeats: a Contemporary Assessment', delivered in Trinity College in January 1986, gave substantial evidence of a more Yeatsian Yeats than he had previously entertained.

In 1977 Deane first outlined his account of Yeats's place in (and placing of) Irish society and culture:

The Protestant Ascendancy in Ireland *is now and has for long been* [emphasis added] a predominantly bourgeois social formation. . . (Ronsley p. 320)

Certainly, by *Celtic Revivals* (1985) he had modified his position, writing there that

Yeats's account of the Anglo-Irish tradition blurs an important distinction between the terms 'aristocracy' and 'Ascendancy'. Had he known a little more about the eighteenth century, he would have recognized that the Protestant Ascendancy was, *then and since* [emphasis added], a predominantly bourgeois social formation. The Anglo-Irish were held in contempt by the Irish-speaking masses as people of no blood, without lineage and with nothing to recommend them other than the success of their Hanoverian cause over that of the Jacobites. This is evident in the poetry of men such as Daithi O Bruadair and Aodaghain O Rathaille who lived through the first and most painful phase of the Whig Settlement in Ireland. (p. 30)

This is a good deal more satisfactory, though one still finds no priority of history over myth in an argument which discovers a response to Hanoverian success (George I arrived in 1714) in the poetry of O Bruadair (died 1698). Moreover, the Gaelic poets' obsession with lineage has replaced the Yeatsian concern with breeding, and in no sense does this apparent distinguishing of the Protestant Ascendancy – a century before its conception – from an aristocracy engage with the economic or social actualities of class. In the absence, one might say the calculated and callous absence of any initiative political or intellectual from the British New Left, the implicit radicalism of the *Atlantis* years lapses into an amalgam of Lévi-Strauss structuralism and the unexamined denominational labels. The altering status of the southern state, like the inner dynamics of class in Ulster, is unable to command attention in such critical systems.

## iv. Conor Cruise O'Brien Revisited

We left Dr O'Brien quite a long time ago, and he has spent much of the intervening period urging the untrammelled rightness of Ulster Unionist rejection of the Anglo-Irish accord. In January 1986 he claimed that he could not assuage Unionist fears because he shared them, and though this may seem remote from sublime thoughts on French Catholic fiction it does doubtless reflect *some* of the conflicts really occuring in the back streets of our cities. Yet the distance between the critic and columnist is deceptive. The critic has told us, in *States of Ireland* (1972), how differences of opinion concerning the advisability of his parents' marrying 'left in this extended family, under the surface, an emotional division which tended to reflect wider divisions in the society' (p. 83). These wider divisions, one hardly needs to be told, were and are sectarian. Though Frank Cruise O'Brien was not a Protestant he was constantly in touch with that element:

he worked with a Protestant, Guy Lloyd, on an edition of Lecky's *Rise of Rationalism in Europe*. He understood Protestant fears about Catholic domination in an independent Ireland, because he shared these fears. (p.84)

Just as the younger Cruise O'Brien's words of 1986 echo his father's at the beginning of the century, so rationalism (including agnosticism) and Protestantism stand in for each other in the Irish scheme of things. For the author of a book concerned with 'imaginative patterns in a group of modern Catholic writers', such elisions are potent things. The parental past emerges in middle age, mutely hinting that this crisis of 1986 somehow *is* that earlier crisis. The political background to the Cruise O'Brien family was the fall of Parnell, and then later, the hijacking of the reunited Irish Party's position by Pearse's armed republicans in 1916. In the final chapter of *Maria Cross* O'Brien had suggested that the clue to understanding the English authors he discussed lay in assessing 'the last years of the nineteenth century', a crucial historic period characterized by the ultimate disintegration of that emphasis on the 'rational faculties' which had begun (perhaps) with the French Revolution. In relation to the pervasive rigidity of thinking displayed by intellectuals as seemingly different as

O'Brien himself, Edna Longley and Seamus Deane – a rigidity grounded in sectarian division – the same period offers the possibility of an explanation.

While the ideology of Protestant Ascendancy had provided one means whereby the reality of class conflict was displaced and distorted, the social consequences of the *Ne Temere* decree of 1907 reinforced with ecclesiastical authority a sense of absolute division that had previously been experienced as relative (and relating) *difference*. Marriage and the laws concerning inheritance had been a major concern of the original Ascendants in 1792, but in the nineteenth century the practice was well established whereby sons followed the denomination of the father in a mixed marriage, and daughters followed the mother. The Kerry playwright, George Fitzmaurice, is eloquent on this topic of pre-1907 mixed marriages, his father having been a Church of Ireland rector and his mother a Catholic. When Protestant Ascendancy was entering the classic phase of its elegaic self-celebration as cultural compensation for the loss of power, the papal decree on marriage provided the essential second proposition to the binary sociology upon which twentieth-century Ireland has been founded.

With this kind of shifting political and ecclesiastical background, the psychic drama of a Christmas garden is potent, bringing together the locus of the Fall and the time of the Incarnation. That of December 1927 is significant precisely because it unfolds an origin-myth of the Irish State and sub-state whose successors today are (the Republic of) Ireland and (the United Kingdom of Great Britain and) Northern Ireland. Those brackets are awkward, but indicative of the encaged and disabling social existence available as a consequence today. And while any summary is incomplete, it may not be too much to suggest that Conor Cruise O'Brien's loyalty to the Protestant cause proceeds from what is symbolized in the same psychic drama, whereby the succeeding son vindicates the defeated father's cause through a theology of guilt and redemption sanctioned by the mother. The fundamental example of Lévi-Strauss's analysis was, after all, the story of Oedipus. In such a surrogate politics, if we are – any of us in Ireland – permitted to be related, it is 'through Maria Cross'.

O'Brien's critical enterprise thus emerges as less eccentric and inconsistent than originally seemed likely, and its pattern fits the ideological contradictions of the political as well as intellectual background just indicated. At one level, he meets Declan Kiberd's requirements for an Irish intellectual; at another he is disabled by this weight of qualification. Heaney, on the other hand, whose family is seemingly *ur*-native and Catholic, emerges from an overlapping of historic and pedagogic codes which apparently gives him a disciplined access to the variable quantum of subjectivity that runs through the Irish imagination. The two most intriguing intellectual figures of contemporary Irish debate thus disinter themselves from origins which are marked by overdetermined and painfully enfolded lines.

## v.'Our rivals now are ended'

I sense a rumbling triumphalist accusation whereby I am seen as minimizing in the Catholic instance *(Ne Temere)* the divisive consequences I dwell upon at length in the Protestant instance (Ascendancy). But there are several distinguishing features between the two codes of division. First, in relation to marriage the papal decree sought to encourage assimilation and continuity of belief, where the Protestant Ascendancy debates of 1792 explicitly cited marriage as an area through which Catholics must not be assimilated to the dominant elite. Property was the prime consideration then, and it is touching to note the honesty with which the anti-divorce lobby in 1986 acknowledge rights of inheritance as the theological *ne plus ultra* still. More importantly, *Ne Temere* is an explicit, citable proposition (however authoritarian) whereas Protestant Ascendancy remained a blurred spectrum of values, strategies and prejudices in which definition (whether of class or creed) was not preferred to the distortions of a reductive binary schema.

On the other hand, the violence which threatens is a common feature in the western hemisphere – also the southern one. The methods of the IRA, and those of the UDA, have analogues in the American present (or the French future) as well as in the Irish past. To speak, as we have spoken, of the

Ulster situation providing an *undeniable* background of deprivation against which Heaney's poetic of regeneration in loss is brutally to discount conditions in Soweto, Buenos Aires and Iran. If we are persuaded to see an imminent battle here in terms of a still phosphorescent history, it is not unconnected with the manner in which critical debate has been cast in the iron categories I hope I have exposed to view. Social division by denomination is ultimately a form of ancestor-worship; though we note the absence of theological content in Gerry Adams and Andy Tyrie, we substitute an even more absurd irrationalism than ever Transubstantiation or the Westminster Confession was. Social division by denomination replaces the future with the past. Nevertheless, recognition of this depressing pattern brings with it the possibility of changing it. Not an immediate prospect of total change to be sure, but the possibility nonetheless of working towards the dissolution of that frozen sociology of Gog and Magog, Big-Endians and Little-Endians, Them and Us.

What are the means to this end? If we are to have a fully radical literary history we have to find new ways to sustain the critique of a culture which, while hyping every brand of tradition, is in steady crisis. One priority I would commend is the disentagling of two very different commitments – to politics *per se,* to 'the community' and all that weasel-word connotes today. The poetry of Thomas Kinsella has not featured in *The Battle of the Books* largely because it avoids the identification of community and *polis* so fatally active in these disputes. And so Kinsella becomes the focal point for an argument counter to the present one, an argument in which his technique of Alexandrian commentary, his recurrent image of falling, the necropolis of his setting, his use of visual devices as a means of revealing the materiality of the poetic word – in which all this would be shown as part of a quite different aesthetic. And this could bring other things within view, the poetry (too neglected here) of Derek Mahon, John Banville's fiction and, at last, Samuel Beckett. Delayed gratification is not always a folly. *The Battle of the Books* has been concerned essentially with rival forms of populism, middle-class to be sure, but a populism eagerly resistant to so fundamental a question as this: to whom, and by what means, can one present the theme of *the disappearance of the the public?* For through this general theme of Fredric Jameson's, we can discern disturbingly neglected questions of a local kind – who reads Seamus Heaney's poems and with what consequences; to what intellectual/ideological constituency is Cruise O'Brien attached; what kind of performance has *Field Day* in mind for us; why does C. J. Haughey want to be managing director of the Culture Industry?

If there has been a necessary recourse to history in this essay on contemporary debates, its justification is that the past contains, indeed *detains*, not answers but unasked questions. Not all of these can be even listed here, but one unavoidable issue relates to the need for a theory of colonialism which surpasses *Coral Island* in complexity. The crucial years of that 'long Edwardianism' referred to in the preface saw the transformation of the imperial powers through World War, years which brought not only Bolshevism in Russia, Spartacus in Germany and the Republic of Councils in Hungary but – all too swiftly – counter-revolution in the West. It was in this long Edwardian massacre that the Irish middle classes survived, a point eloquently repressed in Frank McGuinness's much-lauded and class-discussing play, *Behold the Sons of Ulster Marching towards the Somme.*

There remain today concealed yet undeniable vectors of our culture for which the concept of 'debate' is either outmoded or premature. Not all of these vectors possess the same magnitude nor head in the same direction, but they deserve attention as distinctly different from the shared ground of *Field Day,* Edna Longley, Terence Brown and company. I would instance the kind of theatre in which Olwyn Fouere is involved, the music of Frank Corcoran, painting from the Oliver Dowling Gallery (Mary Fitzgerald, Felim Egan, the late Cecil King). Fifty years after Beckett wrote to Axel Kaun, his proposal in relation to language is still a provocation:

To bore one hole after another in it, until what lurks behind it – be it something or nothing – begins to seep through; I cannot imagine a higher goal for a writer today. Or is literature alone to remain behind in the old lazy ways that have been so long abandoned by music and painting? (9 July 1937. *Disjecta,* p. 172: text originally in German)

Though it is usual to relate Heaney either to Yeats or Joyce, it might make more sense to consider him with Samuel Beckett. For it is in Beckett's work – as Theodor Adorno indicated, reading *Endgame* as crucially a post-war work – that the modern disintegration of a particular subject/object construct finds one of its most delicate aesthetic forms. The excess/deficiency of the subject in Heaney's poems, 'Toome' and 'Broagh', requires reading in a literary history which does not omit *Endgame*. We noted earlier that there were social determinants affecting Heaney's work, one of these evident through the power of longing for accommodation in an order which, in rebutting him, cancelled and intensified that longing. Beckett's upbringing and gradual outgoing involved tensions which, given the differences between Dublin in the 1920s and Ulster forty years later, deserve comparison with Heaney's. Ultimately, the comparison would call forth a book for which the cumbersome title would be *The Ma(s)king of the Irish Middle Class*. For therein lies the whole dispute, the prolonged refusal of Irish literary history to acknowledge the bourgeois character of its material.

# Select Bibliography

Generally, whenever material from a newspaper or magazine was quoted, sufficient information (date, issue number or whatever) was provided on the text to enable the reader to follow up the source. For books quoted, the page-number appeared after each quotation, and now fuller details of publication are provided below. A few titles have been added simply because they are relevant. An asterisk indicates a title which contains further material by the present writer.

Theodor W. Adorno, *The Jargon of Authenticity*. London: Routledge, 1973.

J. C. Beckett, *The Anglo-Irish Tradition*. London: Faber, 1976.

Samuel Beckett, *Disjecta,* London: Calder, 1983.

Walter Benjamin, *The Origins of German Tragic Drama*. London: New Left Books, 1977.

Terence Brown, *Ireland, a Social and Cultural History 1922-79.* [n.p.] Fontana, 1981. (Rev. ed., with postscript, 1985).

——, *Northern Voices: Poets from Ulster*. Dublin: Gill and Macmillan, 1975.

Peter Costello, *The Heart Grown Brutal; the Irish Revolution in Literature from 1891 to 1939*. Dublin: Gill and Macmillan, 1978.

Conor Cruise-O'Brien, *Camus*. [n.p.]: Fontana, 1970.

——, *Maria Cross: Imaginative Patterns in a Group of Modern Catholic Writers*. London: Chatto & Windus, 1954.

——, *States of Ireland*. London: Hutchinson, 1972.

——, *Writers and Politics*. London: Chatto and Windus, 1965.

L. M. Cullen, *The Emergence of Modern Ireland 1600-1900*. London: Batsford, 1981.

*Gerald Dawe and Edna Longley, *Across a Roaring Hill: the Protestant Imagination in Modern Ireland*. Belfast: Blackstaff, 1985.

Seamus Deane, *Celtic Revivals: Essays in Modern Irish Literature 1880-1980*. London: Faber, 1985.

——. *et al. Ireland's Field Day*. London: Hutchinson, 1985. (Contains the first six pamphlets and a postscript by Denis Donoghue: for details of the pamphlets' original publication, see p. 54 above.)

John Wilson Foster, *Forces and Themes in Ulster Fiction*. Dublin: Gill and Macmillan, 1974.

*Jeremy Hawthorn, *Narrative from Malory to Motion Pictures*. London: Edward Arnold, 1985.

Fredric Jameson, *Marxism and Form: Twentieth-Century Dialectical Theories of Literature*. Princeton: Princeton Univ. Press, 1971.

——, *The Political Unconscious: Narrative as a Socially Symbolic Act*. London: Methuen, 1981.

Martin Jay, *The Dialectical Imagination: a History of the Frankfurt School and the Institute of Social Research 1923-1950*. London: Heinemann, 1973.

A. N. Jeffares and K.G.W. Cross, *In Excited Reverie: a Centenary Tribute to William Butler Yeats 1865-1939*. London: Macmillan, 1965.

Dillon Johnston, *Irish Poetry Since Joyce*. Mountrath: Dolmen; Notre Dame: Univ. of Notre Dame Press, 1985.

Richard Kearney, *Dialogues with Contemporary Continental Thinkers; the Phenomenological Heritage*. Manchester: Manchester Univ. Press, 1984.

——, (ed.) *The Irish Mind: Exploring Intellectual Traditions*. Dublin: Wolfhound Press, 1985.

Thomas Kinsella (and W.B. Yeats), *Davis, Mangan, Ferguson? Tradition and the Irish Writer*. Dublin: Dolmen Press, 1970.

Frank Lentricchia, *After the New Criticism*. London: Athlone Press, 1980.

——, *Criticism and Social Change*. Chicago: Univ. of Chicago Press, 1983.

F. S. L. Lyons, *Culture and Anarchy in Ireland 1890-1939*. Oxford: Clarendon Press, 1979.

W. J. Mc Cormack, *Ascendancy and Tradition in Anglo-Irish Literary History from 1789 to 1939*. Oxford: Clarendon Press, 1985.

——, *Sheridan Le Fanu and Victorian Ireland*. Oxford: Clarendon Press, 1980.

★ ——, (ed.), *A Festschrift for Francis Stuart on his Seventieth Birthday*. Dublin: Dolmen Press, 1972.

★ ——, (ed. with Alistair Stead), *James Joyce and Modern Literature*. London, Boston: Routledge, 1982.

——, 'Seeing Darkly: Notes on Beckett and Adorno', *Hermathena*, No. CXLI, Winter 1986.

Oliver MacDonagh, *Ireland: the Union and its Aftermath*. (2nd ed.) London: Allen & Unwin, 1977.

——, *States of Mind: a Study of Anglo-Irish Conflict 1780-1980*. London: Allen & Unwin, 1983.

Tom Nairn, *The Break-up of Britain: Crisis and Neo-Nationalism*. (2nd. ed.) London: Verso Books, 1981.

Liam de Paor, *Divided Ulster*. (2nd ed.) Harmondsworth: Penguin Books, 1971.

Tom Paulin, *Ireland and the English Crisis*. Newcastle Upon Tyne: Bloodaxe Books, 1984.

Joseph Ronsley, (ed.) *Myth and Reality in Irish Literature*. Waterloo (Ontario): Wilfrid Laurier Univ. Press, 1977.

Edward Said, *Orientalism*. London: Routledge, 1978.

——, *The World, the Text, and the Critic*. Cambridge (Mass.): Harvard U.P., 1983.

Francis Shaw, 'The Canon of Irish History – A Challenge', *Studies*, vol. XLI, summer 1972.

★Andrew Swarbrick, (ed.) *The Art of Oliver Goldsmith*. London: Vision Press, 1984.

Elizabeth Young-Bruehl and Robert Hogan, *Conor Cruise O'Brien; an Appraisal*. Newark: Proscenium Press, 1974.

# Index

'Inverted commas' indicate discussion, at least under one entry, of a topic in conceptual or linguistic terms. All names of the Mac/Mc type are filed as if beginning Mc.

93